UNHOOKED

"*Unhooked* is a book that needed to be written. The opioid epidemic is the public health crisis of our lifetime. There is no shortage of advocacy groups seeking the allocation of financial resources to treat this crisis. Those of us in the trenches realize that if all of the advocates' pleas for financial resources are answered, societally we do not have the trained staff and other resources to meet the need. Chris and Jill examine a barrier that few commentators choose to tackle in the public debate, an ̶ ̶ ̶ ̶ ̶ ̶ spotty social safety net that var ̶ ̶ ̶ ̶ : lines and across varying geogr ̶ ̶ ̶ ction treatment can be delive ̶ ̶ ̶ population health management model, it will remain difficult to consistently produce successful outcomes."

Drew Rothermel, CEO, BRC Healthcare

"Before the attention of society was shifted to the coronavirus pandemic, we had already had a crisis of substance use disorders affecting many of our communities and our circle of friends and family. Regardless of your level of connection to this topic, personal or professional, I hope you find this book to be informative, engaging, and empowering. Both Jill and Chris make the case for why we need to act and how we can take steps to improve our healthcare delivery systems."

Mark Fung, MD, PhD, Vice Chair for Population Health, Department of Pathology and Laboratory Medicine, The University of Vermont Health Network

CHRIS POWELL &
JILL S. WARRINGTON, MD, PhD

UNHOOKED

Tackling Opioid Addiction and Behavioral
Health Conditions through a Population Health Model

Published by Advantage, Charleston, South Carolina.
Member of Advantage Media Group.

ADVANTAGE is a registered trademark, and the Advantage colophon is a trademark of Advantage Media Group, Inc.

Printed in the United States of America.

10 9 8 7 6 5 4 3 2 1

ISBN: 978-1-64225-171-5
LCCN: 2021922639

Cover design by Megan Elger.
Layout design by Wesley Strickland.

This publication is designed to provide accurate and authoritative information in regard to the subject matter covered. It is sold with the understanding that the publisher is not engaged in rendering legal, accounting, or other professional services. If legal advice or other expert assistance is required, the services of a competent professional person should be sought.

Advantage Media Group is proud to be a part of the Tree Neutral® program. Tree Neutral offsets the number of trees consumed in the production and printing of this book by taking proactive steps such as planting trees in direct proportion to the number of trees used to print books. To learn more about Tree Neutral, please visit www.treeneutral.com.

Advantage Media Group is a publisher of business, self-improvement, and professional development books and online learning. We help entrepreneurs, business leaders, and professionals share their Stories, Passion, and Knowledge to help others Learn & Grow. Do you have a manuscript or book idea that you would like us to consider for publishing? Please visit advantagefamily.com.

CONTENTS

ACKNOWLEDGMENTS

We want to thank healthcare professionals who work tirelessly every day to support the substance use disorder (SUD) community. We recognize the daily impact that you have on our patients, the lives of their loved ones, and our communities. We honor your contributions to advancing the field. We have written this work to celebrate you and to recognize the obstacles you face in administering care. We are hopeful for the future—a future in which the stigma for SUD is removed; a future in which clinical care is seamlessly integrated into a holistic approach to the patient; and a future where providers can easily collaborate together for our collective benefit.

We are grateful for the support we have had in writing this work. We want to thank Lisa Canfield, Nate Best, and Olivia Tanksley for their support in writing, editing, and organizing this book. Thank you also to the many politicians, C-suite administrators, providers, persons with SUD, caregivers, and family members who have contributed directly to this work through interviews, insights, and provision of evidence-based practices. We are also so grateful to our colleagues and families for their support throughout this endeavor.

WHO WE ARE

Chris Powell grew up in an alcoholic household, where he experienced the trials and traumas of addiction firsthand. As an adult, he spent his career at the crossroads of healthcare and innovation. He has served as vice president and general manager of GE Healthcare, overseeing the company's efforts in Canada and Central and South America. Chris then served as CEO of Precyse, a health information management and services company that covered medical coding, healthcare education, and a service-enabled technology platform to improve coding and workflow. Becoming CEO at Aspenti Health, Chris recognized the criticality of the work in the field and rallied investors to support a new vision: the application of a population health strategy to the treatment of substance use disorders (SUD). Leveraging a preexisting randomization platform used to support specimen collections and testing, Chris's team created a novel digital service replete with a diagnostic module that supports test ordering and resulting, ICD-10 coding, community event engagement, and protocol management. He also promoted digital educational content development distributed across partner networks and a new population-health analytics program. This vision propelled the company to a new level and provided a powerful and effective service to providers in the region.

Jill Warrington has spent the past twenty-five years in healthcare. Beginning her career as a federally funded MD-PhD student, Jill bridged the clinical and research worlds, recognizing the critical nature of translational medicine and the value of applying research principles to clinical service work. With a PhD in pharmacology, Jill was exposed to the operations of pharmaceutical companies and the principles of laboratory medicine. Through her academic career, she has learned from some of the best at Princeton University, Tufts School of Medicine and Graduate Sciences, Duke University, and now the University of Vermont. Throughout her career, she has brought thought leadership to her endeavors, publishing pioneering research on innovations in SUD and spearheading a number of grant-funding projects in this area. Through her work with Chris at Aspenti Health, where she served as chief medical officer, she collaborated with institutions on bold new approaches to substance-use treatment, helping to introduce new reporting strategies for laboratory-result interpretation; providing countless local, regional, and national presentations; serving as course director for digital educational content development; and championing innovative solutions in the organization, such as the introduction of a transformative testing strategy—known as comprehensive screening—to the field. Further collaborations have involved the following: a mobile unit for specimen collections during the COVID-19 pandemic; the development of a telehealth strategy for observed collections (telecollections); Lean Six Sigma operational and quality efficacies to the laboratory; and the investigation of several offerings to the digital platform, including the incorporation of social determinants of health data and the collaborative helping model. Today she serves as Director of Population Health for the Department of Pathology and Laboratory Medicine at the University of Vermont College of Medicine and as Laboratory Director for the Vermont Department of Health Laboratory.

THE CURRENT STATE OF AFFAIRS

*No one is immune from addiction; it afflicts people
of all ages, races, classes, and professions.*

—PATRICK J. KENNEDY

Communities ravaged. Healthcare facilities overwhelmed. Bank accounts drained, livelihoods lost, and most tragically, a shocking rise in death tolls.

You may think we're describing the impact of the COVID-19 pandemic. And we very well could be. But these circumstances apply to a very different epidemic. An epidemic that in many ways is more insidious and will continue long after this coronavirus outbreak. Unlike COVID-19, where an entire world mobilized to meet this enormous challenge, this epidemic mostly exists in silence, with very limited coordination to halt its explosive growth. Yet, from 1999 through 2018, nearly half a million people have died from its effects, making it seem as though we as a society have gradually come to accept the unacceptable.[1] If you haven't guessed, we are discussing the opioid crisis. Despite our valiant efforts, the epidemic only gets worse: from May 2019 to May 2020, over eighty-one thousand individuals died from drug overdose deaths.

The issue of substance use disorders (SUD, for short) is, simply put, the most pressing ongoing healthcare crisis of our time—and a symptom of our real societal problem: a growing prevalence of behavioral health (BH) conditions. Year after year, the mushrooming of prescription opioid misuse chips away at three critical pillars of our country: our communities, our economy, and our citizens. Despite progress on bringing this problem into the spotlight over the past few years, it continues to haunt every level of our society in harmful and systemic ways. Only a few of the impacts are listed here.

Our Communities

According to the Centers for Disease Control and Prevention (CDC), nearly half a million deaths were attributable to opioid-related overdoses from 1997 to 2017. Approximately twice the number of fatalities were seen from alcohol use during that same time span. In 2016 and 2017, more than 130 people died of opioid overdoses alone (84 percent of all overdose deaths), according to the US Department of Health and Human Services.

Every death is a person, a friend, a coworker, a child, a parent. Every death reverberates across our communities and disrupts the fabric of our society. The impact of SUD is not limited to deaths alone. SUD can disrupt every element of our community health—from ongoing medical conditions to challenges in our workforce to

---

1   "Opioid Data Analysis and Resources," Centers for Disease Control and Prevention, accessed September 1, 2021, https://www.cdc.gov/drugoverdose/data/analysis.html.

public safety. The cost, the loss, and the devastation cannot be fully calculated.

> Every death is a person, a friend, a coworker, a child, a parent.

Our Economy

We contribute billions to SUD treatment annually with insufficient changes in outcome. Each year, we lose billions in workforce productivity from absenteeism and unemployment. The economic life blood of entire towns has been devastated by opioid addiction.

Our Citizens

Patients and their loved ones suffer enormous hardships and not just from the financial burdens of addiction. Many maladies accompany SUD, including hepatitis C, endocarditis, alcohol-related cardiomyopathy, neonatal abstinence syndrome, and cirrhosis, to name a few. Families often experience debilitating dysfunction due to addiction, which all too frequently can directly or indirectly impact generations. Beyond these devastating consequences, these sequelae can have a significant financial impact. For example, we estimate that for every patient with opioid use disorder (OUD), we spend $20,000 on liver diseases alone.

* * *

The national crisis—spanning opioid use, a host of prescribed and illicit drugs, and the silent killer of alcoholism—has been an enormous societal challenge. The burden from the decades-long opioid crisis and the corresponding mental health crisis may be about to expand exponentially, if social media is any indication. If you're a user of Facebook, Instagram, Twitter, or other platforms, you know how many memes have circulated during the COVID-related quarantine about overusing drugs and alcohol because you're stuck at home with nothing to do. Jabs on social media about increased use of drugs and alcohol are really flashing red lights for what our society is going to have to deal with once COVID-19 has been contained or even conquered.

At the time of this writing, our nation is completely overwhelmed managing the influx of coronavirus cases. State and government officials have been tasked with slowing the spread which, in a word, boils down to one mandate: "social distance." The effects of quarantine are individual and can, for some, just be boredom. But, to those most vulnerable and afflicted with addiction, quarantine's effects are detrimental, mounting progressively with each day in isolation. A widely adopted model for successful addiction treatment has yet to reach mass consensus, but all agree that connection to support systems is critical.

The tenets of addiction treatment involve in-person group therapy. During COVID, meeting face-to-face in therapy sessions is postponed. Alcoholics Anonymous (AA) meetings have moved to virtual settings. COVID testing may add more barriers to seeking help. Patients aren't getting urine testing. Some patients may not see their primary care doctor. Many are out of work, anxious, and depressed. While telehealth has demonstrated promise in facilitating access in the space, many providers find it is promoting burnout. For those susceptible to substance misuse, poor mental health and social isolation can be the catalyst to resume use. If you follow the trajectory, there is the real possibility that today's overpowering addiction crisis will explode during the pandemic and we will suffer damages far greater than any of us have yet to experience.

As healthcare stakeholders, we must ask some crucial but uncomfortable questions. In an era when media, academia, Big Pharma, government, payers, and grass roots efforts have loudly addressed the addiction crisis in our country, why is healthcare still so challenged in its effort to manage addiction? Why are we unable to reverse trends seen for decades? How do we take a disease that is so personal and a treatment that is so tailored and scale it for the masses? Is there a way to reframe our entire approach? Can we systemically make a difference to those affected while also preventing a new generation from becoming addicted?

We believe we can.

Many books addressing the addiction crisis have been written. We're not looking to add another dusty volume to library shelves simply to regurgitate information. We've found many books look at the behavioral health crisis with a retrospective lens instead of with an eye to the future. Proactive strategies to solve the crisis are sparse. Books that do speak to solutions too often focus on strategies for individual patients. Few propose ideas that large-scale clinical organizations can implement to create sweeping change.

Instead, our current healthcare system is well equipped to handle addiction episodes—and woefully unprepared to tackle the underlying issues that cause continual relapses. After all, as providers, we understand how to manage overdoses. But is it really treatment when we revive patients in the ED and send them on their way with an expectation that they will follow up with a different provider? These are very challenging settings in which to address a patient's overarching behavioral health issues. This is a costly, time-consuming process that creates uncertain outcomes at best.

But what's preferable? Treating a series of episodic addiction events that are high cost or implementing a long-term behavioral-health-related treatment plan that, if successful, can create a lifetime of wellness? Ultimately, the latter leads to a much lower investment of time and money than repeatedly treating a patient with addiction whose physical ailments will undoubtedly continue to increase over the years.

Think of it this way: If you only treat the physical wounds of a teenage girl who deliberately cuts, she will continue to cut and treatment will only address the wounds themselves. If you can help the young girl heal the *mental* wound that motivates her cutting, you've given her an enormous gift that will ultimately make her happier and healthier. If you can recognize the principles that you are applying for this patient, you can take these findings to others and better manage the population. Those afflicted with SUD can also be given that gift. But because their behavioral health issues are often not fully addressed, their lives can remain stuck in self-destructive loops. All strategies must embrace the larger context in which this disease arises, including larger behavioral health needs—the individual's social determinants of health, their mental health, and the inequities of their circumstances.

In addition to recognizing the context for the development of an individual patient's SUD, we need to consider how we can scale this work beyond the patient in front of us. Each patient is unique, and the individuality of each patient on their road to recovery must be acknowledged and addressed; however, there are systemic standards of care that can inform that customized work. We must transform our approach. While individualized, patient-centered care must prevail, we need to create systematic, population-based strategies to inform this tailored work. This population-based lens will not only help us better manage the patient in front of us but also allow us to bring this work to other providers and patients.

That's why we're writing this book—because something *has* to change. We want to empower that change by going beyond the physical effects of addiction and placing the emphasis where it needs to be—on the patient's well-being. The traditional model of care addresses substance use. Success in treatment is mostly character-ized by abstinence. We need a different set of metrics by which to measure success and a different focus on what constitutes a win. Our mission is to contribute a wholly new framework by which to move us forward.

> Something *has* to change.

* * *

Significant obstacles impede progress in behavioral health treatment. Each stakeholder within the healthcare arena is challenged. Healthcare executives battle to improve outcomes. Reimbursement rates continue to decline, despite pressure to improve care without cost adjustments. Care teams and treatment programs work with limited human capital, experiencing an increase in case load numbers and complexity. The resources are too minimal to adequately deal with this population's presenting challenges.

The dismal reality is this: The industry, as a whole, has developed few standards for care, few coordinated strategies, and few promising prospects for change in SUD patients' behavioral needs. Standards that are in place are too limited and too fragmented to scale or measure progress. We have seen local successes through state or institutional frameworks, such as the Massachusetts model or the hub-and-spoke model; however, even across these remarkable settings, there is little uniformity to the delivery of care and few consensus-based metrics for success. These factors combine to create a tide of negativity or frustration that can lead to burnout—and little to no progress for patients who desperately need change.

Make no mistake about it. There are many regulators, politicians, and policymakers who are anxious to create positive change through increased and redirected funding. The challenge is there is little consensus on how those funds should be deployed, what constitutes the best clinical value, and how to measure success. There is also a dearth of private investment and funding of innovative technologies. Families of individuals afflicted with addiction feel even more helpless. They're screaming for a viable road to recovery so they can return balance to their lives, restore the health of their loved ones, and move forward to a brighter future. Our patients desire and deserve a productive and rewarding professional life, a stable family, loving and supportive friends, and an optimized physical and mental well-being.

As passionate change agents, we, in writing this book, want to see this transform—just as we are certain that you, in reading this, do too. We are all familiar with these bleak scenarios. Many of us have been personally touched by the SUD crisis, cared for loved ones in crisis, or simply felt impassioned by what we read and observe around us. However, despite our best hopes, intentions, and contributions, there is often too little institutional support, too limited national investment, too little bandwidth, and no clear path forward to change behavior when it comes to addiction.

But what if this didn't have to be the reality?

What if we could agree on a framework and create a unified coalition to mitigate poor outcomes, adjust tactical strategies, modify methodologies, and define and track success?

What if we knew what to do and how to do it?

What if we put together an integrated treatment system that actually *worked?*

By crafting successful behavioral-health-centered protocols for SUD patients, we not only have the potential of addressing use but also the consequences that befall this use.

That's why, in this book, we focus on effecting change *at scale*, through the use of innovative, disruptive tactics that clinical institutions can employ to aggressively manage the SUD crisis, going beyond opioid addiction to tackle the threat of addiction writ large.

We believe such an approach is necessary ... and well overdue.

*   *   *

We are not newcomers to this battle. We have dedicated our careers—and our lives—to helping patients overcome potentially deadly addictions.

Our mission is to address population health trends for behavioral health and chronic disease. We collaborate with physicians, payers, treatment centers, and health systems to provide value-based care that optimizes patient outcomes. Our ultimate objective is to serve as stewards of change in the behavioral health space while simultaneously effecting change in the greater healthcare industry's approach to the problem.

We must move beyond the blame game, which limits efforts to confront the addiction crisis and displaces accountability. The more effort spent bickering about who's at fault, the more diluted our approach becomes. We require industry collaboration in formulating effective treatment strategies and effective measures of success and management tools. We are setting out to reinvent how SUD treatment and behavioral healthcare are delivered. We will outline a proactive, overarching plan for promoting a different approach to behavioral health that, with collaborative work, can promote healthier, more productive lives. To us, the most important element of this plan is the formulation and implementation of a universal philosophy for SUD and behavioral healthcare—a road map for caregiving that we all can follow *together*. We are not going to waste time debating which of the many specific treatment methods is best but rather advocate for a big-picture, long-term approach—both to treating individual patients and to systemically transforming treatment modalities.

We recognize the individuality in care and the fact that diversity in treatment strategies will enable us to meet patients where they are. We are not advocating for a one-size-fits-all approach to care. Rather, we are championing common strategies, mechanisms to monitor and evaluate success, individual institutional alignment and integration, and most of all, a commitment to tackle this disease in a comprehensive and collaborative way.

This is a lofty goal but one we must strive for to offset the decades-long damage our society and its citizens have had to endure. To accomplish this, we will emphasize the importance of managing addiction as a chronic disease and investigate what this perspective might teach us about our approach to treatment. By examining analogous chronic diseases—such as diabetes, heart disease, and chronic obstructive pulmonary disease (COPD), for example—we'll underline the importance of adopting holistic, long-term treatment strategies that account for social determinants of health, disease comorbidities, sequelae, and more. We'll also emphasize the power that data has to transform care strategies. We will share the voices of those affected by SUD—patients, their loved ones, doctors, executives, and politicians—all weighing in with their diverse experiences and their thoughts on how the system needs to be fixed. Finally, we propose a disruptive, innovative approach that transcends traditional healthcare inequities, balances institutional checkbooks, brings order to provider workplaces, and enriches patients' lives in sustained recovery and purpose.

We are not the only ones attempting to mitigate this public health emergency. There are many exceptionally talented and brilliant professionals working to combat addiction across many different channels. We are grateful for and humbled by their dedication and hard work. This book's purpose is to unite stakeholders within a common framework that will allow us all to track to consistent targets of success and drive the best possible outcomes for our patients and society. We also hope to encourage others, including those in the private sector, to actively participate in this space because we believe when we all work together effectively, we will be able to drive the greatest impact.

To create viable solutions, we must first thoroughly understand the problem at hand. In our first chapter, we'll explore this overwhelming health crisis in greater detail and provide an overview of just how severe it has become.

Defining Terms and Intent

Throughout this book, we will refer to treatment and patients. With our laser focus on the addiction crisis, this will mean patients with SUD. We recognize that SUD is only one condition in a larger behavioral health context. When we're referring to a broader perspective—including a comprehensive view to span mental health conditions, behavioral health inequities, and social determinants of health—we will acknowledge these behavioral health needs, but otherwise we will mean SUD. Further, we often use illness, condition, and disease interchangeably. Formally, we recognize SUD as a chronic disease, but through quotes and citations, we occasionally lapse into this other terminology. We hope you will indulge us with this, as we recognize that this variation in language may contribute to or be a reflection of the ways in which this disease is managed.

The overall focus of this work is on SUD—spanning both drugs and alcohol. In many cases we focus in on opioids. In particular, opioid use disorder serves as a case study relevant to today's recognized opioid crisis and overdose deaths; however, we recognize that it is one of several forms of substance use–related addictions that plague us today.

CHAPTER ONE

THE GREATEST HEALTHCARE CRISIS OF OUR TIME

Pain is the oldest medical problem and the universal physical affliction of mankind.

—MARCIA MELDRUM, "A Capsule History of Pain Management," 2003

We cover many facts and figures that detail the immensity of America's opioid epidemic. Unfortunately, facts and figures don't tell the whole story. They can't make you *feel* the impact of the overwhelming human tragedies occurring every single day in this country because of SUD. To demonstrate the personal impact, we start with an account from the parents of an SUD victim that reflects the reality of how lives are destroyed every day because of our failure to fully address this crisis.

Jenna was in her first semester of college when, on Christmas Eve, her boyfriend of three years beat her up and she had to go to the emergency room. She had no broken bones or anything, but she did have a broken heart, and the doctor gave her thirty days of OxyContin. That was the beginning of the battle.

I'm not really sure how long it went on with the prescriptions. With the drug, you have to take more and more, because you build up a tolerance. The doctors would give her more, and Jenna would say, "Mom, it's prescribed to me. If the doctor's giving it to me, then it's okay to take." That whole perception of, if your doctor gives it to you, then it's okay. I didn't know what was going on. I just knew that she didn't go to school and I kept trying to get her to go to school. I just thought she was depressed, but she became very addicted to OxyContin. Eventually she knew that this drug owned her and she had to find creative ways to get it through her doctor—she'd say she was having menstrual problems, or her back was bothering her. You start to create your own problems just to get more of the drug.

Jenna's story may resonate with many of us. While providers were likely following the best standards of care at the time and addressing what must have been a traumatic event precipitating a visit to the emergency room, we have all heard too many stories like Jenna's. We are too aware of how these standards of care were deeply rooted in systemic biases that the healthcare system adopted from the 1990s through the 2010s, leading to even further harm.

When she couldn't get the prescriptions anymore, she ended up going to heroin because she was so sick if she didn't get the pills. Sometimes, when she could get the OxyContin, she would sell her pills for fifty dollars a pill, and she could buy five or six bags of heroin because heroin was so cheap and the demand for the OxyContin was so high. Finally, one day I said, "Jenna, what is going on? You're using drugs, I know you're using drugs. So, what are you using?" And she just looked at me and she said, "Heroin."

I felt at that moment there had been a knife stabbed in my heart because I heard the horror stories that heroin is just … you can't get away from it.

I went to my husband Greg and I was like, "Oh my God, what do we do? I don't know what to do!" They had a meeting once a week for families that were dealing with this, and I remember Greg saying, "Well, we can't go there because everybody knows us." At that point I was so desperate I didn't care who knew us because we just needed help.

We walked into that meeting and we walked out different people because everybody in there was just like us going through the same thing. We thought we were the only ones.

Like many families, Jenna's parents not only needed to support Jenna in her journey to recovery but also faced the stigma that surrounds this disease. Fortunately, they were able to find others with a common experience. Unfortunately, for others, this serves as a crucial impediment to seeking care. While Jenna's parents found some individuals in the community to welcome them, an ongoing supportive infrastructure was lacking.

We wanted to continue with rehab. But the problem is, when Jenna would come home and say, "I'm so sick of this, I just want to go get help," I would desperately call around and there would never be a bed open. I found out pretty quickly I couldn't depend on the state. One time we waited a week, and in the meantime, I was buying stuff for her on the streets—Suboxone—so she wouldn't be sick and so I could get her through to get into rehab. Another time we were waiting to go and they said, "Okay, you can come in this time." And we started going down and they called and said they didn't have the bed available because the person that was going to leave had said something about suicide. So that day I called a place in New Hampshire and they did an intake on the phone and we got her in.

She would go to rehab, and she would do well if she stayed. Sometimes at the end she didn't stay because when she started getting sober, she could really feel the pain and the trauma, and then she would run.

We went to like twenty rehabs over six years, most of them out of the state, just because of not having resources here. And we'd say, "There's nobody out there, there's nobody out there to help. These doctors created this problem, and now they're not giving us any resource to fix it." Even when she started to make the steps in the right direction, she could only stay thirty days in rehab, because our insurance didn't pay for any more than that. And then we would bring her home to the same place … and those dealers would be right back there in a second.

The last time she went to New Hampshire, we said, "You're not coming home. You're going to have to stay in New Hampshire." Because what's the definition of insanity? Doing the same thing over and over and getting the same results. So she stayed in New Hampshire in a sober house, and it was the best thing. She finally found peace, and she was working her steps. They took away her phone, television, all of that. And then as she graduated to the next phase, they gave it back.

Many with SUD share the same experience of entering and reentering treatment. It's so commonplace that it might be considered part of the disease. What if this frequent shuffling across organizations weren't the norm? What if a single institution were able to support a patient in their journey, holding on to and tracking alumni to the same extent that our colleges can find us across the globe whenever their annual fundraising event arises? We submit that our patients and their families might find a less disruptive journey toward recovery.

Then one of her dealers reached out to her and said, "Hey, I need some closure," because they were romantically involved. And she was working on her fourth step, which is to go through and deal with your traumas. So he met her at the sober home, and then she got in the car with him to talk to him, and he never let her out of the car. She texted me, "Help me, he won't let me out." Greg and I said we were going to call the police, but she said, "You can't call the police because I'm with this gang, and we're in a stolen car, and we have $50,000 worth of drugs and guns. They would throw me in jail, and I haven't done anything wrong."

She finally pinged me when she got to Orange, Vermont. It was Sunday night, Greg and I were in Costa Rica, so it's not like I could call my mom or her brother and say, "Hey, go get Jenna at this drug house." I knew they had guns, and I couldn't put any of my family at risk. I couldn't get anyone to get her. No taxi, no Uber or whatever. She texted me, "They're going to try to kill me." They ended up giving her 100 percent fentanyl. And they did.

—Greg and Dawn Tetro, Founders, Jenna's House

Greg and Dawn's heartbreaking story is far from unique. While researching this book, we found no shortage of personal accounts from providers, patients, and their families that reflected the severity of a situation that often seems hopeless. In his award-winning book *Dreamland*, author Sam Quinones's incisive, on-the-ground reporting reflects the desperate times devastating each community. As one of his subjects puts it, "I no longer judge drug addicts."[2]

Neither should we. The opioid crisis reflects massive behavioral health issues within our society that must be addressed, and it's clear that it's not going away anytime soon.

As seen with the current addiction epidemic, opioid misuse has launched addiction numbers into the stratosphere, to the point where a majority of us are touched by tragedy. According to American Addiction Centers, odds are that at least 54 percent of those reading this book know someone who has died from a drug overdose. At least 31 percent of you regarded that individual as a friend.

---

2   Sam Quinones, *Dreamland* (Bloomsbury, 2015).

Relationship to the Deceased

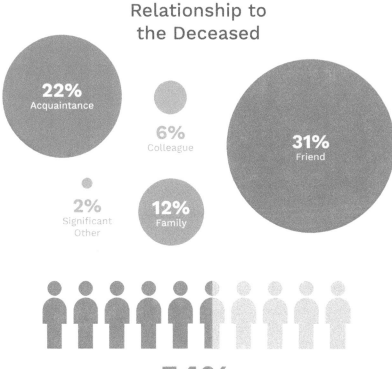

54%
of people know someone who
has died from a drug overdose

1/3
of Americans will have a friend
who dies from an overdose

Modified from American Addiction Centers

Close to a third of us have experienced a tragic personal loss as a result of the current opioid crisis.

With the loss experienced by our nation, the opioid epidemic was declared a public health emergency on October 16, 2017. Its toll has been felt by people of all ages and in every sociodemographic group, from rural shotgun shacks to the well-off country club set. Its insidious reach has even put pressure on our politicians, many of whom used opioid addiction as a campaign issue in 2018. The ripple effects of this epidemic have been truly devastating—and so are the numbers involved:

> Opioid misuse has launched addiction numbers into the stratosphere, to the point where a majority of us are touched by tragedy.

- Opioid misuse cost the US more than $2.5 trillion from 2015 to 2018 (White House Council of Economic Advisors).

- One in eight Emergency Department (ED) visits are attributable to mental health– or substance use–related causes. An SUD diagnosis doubles one's chance of ending up at a clinic or a hospital (Agency for Healthcare Research and Quality).

- Some 11.3 million people misuse prescription meds annually (2017 National Survey on Drug Use and Health).

- The annual economic burden of prescription opioid misuse is $78.5 billion per year nationally, spanning healthcare costs, work-productivity impact, treatment, and criminal justice efforts (National Institute on Drug Abuse, 2013).

Treatment isn't just needed to handle overdoses and other immediate effects of SUD. Treatment can also mitigate negative clinical outcomes, such as HIV, endocarditis, hepatitis B and C, respiratory depression, suicide, cirrhosis and liver cancer, and delirium and comas. Severe health problems, such as neonatal abstinence syndrome and/or intrauterine growth restriction (IUGR), can also evolve for children of patients with SUD.

Overlapping physical and mental health needs can complicate care delivery in confines of an outpatient setting, where the time allotted may be as little as fifteen minutes. In the inpatient setting, the most acute medical needs may place a lower prioritization on their SUD care and detoxification.

Mitigate & Manage Disease Complications

Individual Health Concerns

Endocarditis
Sepsis
Myositis
Osteomyelitis
Cellulitis
Hepatitis B, C & HIV
Cirrhosis
Hepatocellular Carcinoma
Lung Damage
Pulmonary Edema
Respiratory Depression
Suicide
Trauma
Intestinal Rupture
Pruritus
Acute Overdoses
Prolonged QT Interval
Myoclonus
Paralytic Ileus
Shifts in Serum Proteins
    or Antibodies
Falls & Fractures
Hypogonadism
Opioid-Induced Sedation
Motor Vehicle Accidents
Occupational Accidents
Withdrawal Symptoms
Co-Misuse of Alcohol or
    Respiratory Depressants

Common Psychiatric Comorbidities

Anxiety & Mood Disorders
Schizophrenia
Bipolar Disorder
Major Depressive Disorder
Conduct Disorders
Post-Traumatic Stress Disorder

Neonatal Health Concerns

Neonatal Abstinence Syndrome
Congenital Heart Defects
Neonatal Gastroschisis
Intrauterine Growth Restriction
Stillbirth

SUD further challenges the quality of life of patients contending with this diagnosis. Patients can find their lives falling apart at the seams. They may lose their jobs, become estranged from their valuable support system of friends and family, and find themselves at the mercy of our criminal justice department.

We assert that the transition in approach from considering SUD an "affliction" to viewing this condition as a chronic disease will mobilize the healthcare ecosystem to drive better outcomes, reduce costs, and greatly increase access to services.

While we will spend the rest of the book looking forward to provide a vision of how addiction care can be supported in our country, we are, in this chapter only, taking a brief look back at the history of the opioid crisis. We believe this look back is warranted to demonstrate how pervasive and persistent opioid addiction has been throughout our country's entire history, with a very clear pattern of getting a spike in the misuse of one substance under control, only to have another take center stage in its place. While this material is well covered in many resources, its inclusion here should provide a brief context for those less familiar with the topic.

The History of Our Opioid Crisis

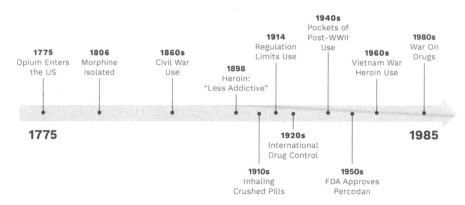

The opioid crisis takes a heavy toll on virtually every aspect of our country. Its origins are as old as that of America itself.

Even before America declared independence, opioids had come to its shores. Opium had reached the US by 1775, though some sources suggest it was present throughout the colonial era. Such storied names as Benjamin Franklin and Alexander Hamilton used it to treat pain. Opiates became more widely used by the early 1800s, when morphine was isolated and hailed as a wonder drug. After all, the new medication could handle the symptoms of everything from headaches to asthma to gastrointestinal diseases to the delirium tremens experienced by alcoholics. Although morphine cured nothing, it seemed to relieve everything. "Doctors were really impressed by the speedy results they got," says David T. Courtwright, author of *Dark Paradise: A History of Opiate Addiction in America.* "It's almost as if someone had handed them a magic wand."[3]

After the Civil War, that magic turned dark. Scores of wounded soldiers returned home hooked on morphine. The Union Army alone issued nearly 10 million opium pills to its troops, not to mention 2.8 million ounces of opium powders and tinctures. Addiction rates suddenly soared, and by 1895, one in two hundred Americans had developed a dependence on morphine as well as opium powders. Women constituted 60 percent of that afflicted group because doctors began to liberally prescribe opioids to relieve menstrual cramps.

The medical community, recognizing the seriousness of this first opioid epidemic, worked to develop what was initially thought to be a far less addictive alternative that still packed a pain-relieving punch. In 1898, they came up with what they considered to be a perfect substitute drug.

---

3   Erick Trickey, "Inside the Story of America's 19th-Century Opiate Addiction," *Smithsonian*, January 4, 2018, https://www.smithsonianmag.com/history/inside-story-americas-19th-century-opiate-addiction-180967673/.

Heroin.

Heroin did not serve our nation's addiction well. Not only was heroin also addictive, but it also possessed twice the potency of morphine, the drug it was designed to "protect" us from. Sold as an over-the-counter remedy after its inception, it helped instigate yet another spike in addiction rates.

The addiction explosion became a national scandal, as users began snorting crushed opioid pills. In 1909, the US Congress banned all imports of opium. In 1914, they passed the Harrison Narcotic Act, which regulated opioid use to such an extent that it was virtually a prohibition. For decades, opioids continued to be used as an underground drug through the black market. During the Vietnam War, the number of heroin users skyrocketed, as the drug flowed freely within South Vietnamese borders. Once again, our soldiers were on the front lines of a battle that was almost impossible to win, as they became the victims of readily available and highly addictive substances. "Tens of thousands of soldiers are going back as walking time bombs," said a military officer at the time. "And the sad thing is that there is no real program under way, despite what my superiors say, to salvage these guys."[4]

---

4   Alvin M. Shuster, "G.I. Heroin Addiction Epidemic in Vietnam," *New York Times*, May 16, 1971, https://www.nytimes.com/1971/05/16/archives/gi-heroin-addiction-epidemic-in-vietnam-gi-heroin-addiction-is.html.

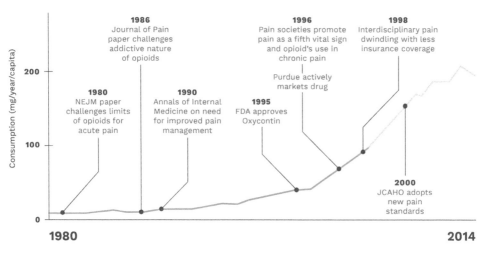

As the Vietnam War wound down, another war ramped up—the US government's so-called War on Drugs. On October 27, 1970, Congress passed the Comprehensive Drug Abuse Prevention and Control Act of 1970, which categorized controlled substances based on medicinal use and addiction potential. In 1973, the Drug Enforcement Agency (DEA) was created under the Nixon administration.

It wasn't until the Reagan administration, in the 1980s, that the clampdown really began. In the first term of Reagan's presidency, the Comprehensive Crime Control Act of 1984 passed, which expanded penalties toward cannabis possession, establishing a federal system of mandatory minimum sentences and procedures for civil asset forfeiture. From 1980 to 1984, the annual federal budget of the FBI's drug enforcement units skyrocketed from eight million to ninety-five million. As a result, America's incarceration rates mushroomed.

A new and very different war began. A war on pain.

In the 1980s, as the War on Drugs heightened, the medical community was concurrently seeking tools in pain management, as patients sought relief from their chronic pain issues. In the late nineties, promoted by the marketing of opioid pills and providers' desire to comfort patients, the idea of declaring pain as "the fifth vital sign" took root. Suddenly, the evaluation of pain became a requirement for proper patient care, as important and basic as the assessment and management of temperature, blood pressure, respiratory rate, and heart rate.

Suddenly, opioids were right back in the mix.

THE BEGINNINGS OF OUR CURRENT CRISIS

Just as heroin was hailed as a major medical breakthrough in the late eighteenth century, so too was opioid-based OxyContin when it gained FDA approval in 1995. OxyContin was seen as a long-lasting narcotic that would effectively treat moderate to severe pain. Like morphine and heroin before it, the new drug immediately sold like gangbusters.

What could go wrong?

Everything, it turned out. Purdue Pharma, the drug's manufacturer, saw it had a winner on its hands and aggressively marketed Oxy. Purdue Pharma's marketing campaign targeted physicians, seeking to alter prescribing practices.

Sales teams with large bonuses were deployed; patient starter coupons distributing free drugs were used; and physicians were provided with swag advertising OxyContin. Since this was a time when the average American's health insurance coverage began to decline, Oxy was regarded by many prescribers as an easy solution for patients' chronic pain problems. As they say, the road to hell is paved with good intentions, and unfortu-

> What could go wrong? Everything, it turned out.

nately, the seeds of our current public health emergency were planted with each and every Oxy prescription.

Purdue Pharma was one of many companies implicated in this sale and distribution of opioids during this time. A few of the prominent companies implicated included the opioid manufacturer Johnson & Johnson; distributors such as McKesson, Cardinal Health, and AmerisourceBergen; the consulting firm McKinsey & Company; and dispensaries such as Walmart.

FROM 1998 PURDUE PHARMA MARKETING VIDEO

"Once you found the right doctor and have told him or her about your pain don't be afraid to take what they give you. Often, it will be an opioid medication. Some patients may be afraid of taking opioids because they are perceived as too strong or addictive. But that is far from actual fact. Less than 1% of patients taking opioids actually become addicted."

In reality, according to the National Institute on Drug Abuse, "Roughly 21 to 29 percent of patients prescribed opioids for chronic pain misuse them."

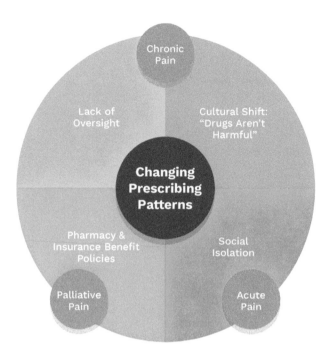

While one of the most influential factors was the liberalization of opioid prescribing patterns, there were other contributors worth mentioning. The opioid epidemic occurred against a backdrop of insufficient oversight, pharmacy and insurance benefit policies that may have incentivized use of drugs, and a cultural shift in the belief that prescribed drugs are not harmful.

Unfortunately, the rise in opioid prescriptions did not always correspond to a patient's actual medical needs. In some states, like Florida, there was a boom in so-called pain clinics, built specifically to be cash cows and little more. "Patients" could simply walk in the door and easily obtain the pills they were after, just by paying for a perfunctory doctor appointment.

At the same time, increasing societal fragmentation and decreasing social connectedness contributed to the rise in addiction as well as other mental health disorders, as more and more sought solace in pills instead of other people. Meanwhile, many of America's traditional support systems grew weaker as income inequality mushroomed and put more pressure on lower income households, who increasingly sought refuge in painkillers to relieve stress and anxiety. From 1999 through 2019, the number of prescribed drugs to patients *doubled.*[5]

While the past two years have seen a rash of settlements and lawsuits implicating some of the companies most responsible for supporting the opioid crisis, the extent of the damage cannot be quantified and the decades-long ensuing crisis still haunts us to this day.

THE THREE WAVES OF THE OPIOID CRISIS

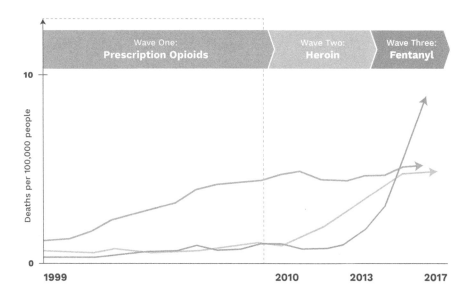

To complete our brief tour through history, we need to address the circumstances of the current crisis. As noted before, we are reviewing history for this chapter only and will quickly turn to a more productive discussion of future opportunities and solutions.

---

5   Rabah Kamal, Cynthia Cox, and Daniel McDermott, "What Are the Recent and Forecasted Trends in Prescription Drug Spending?" Peterson-Kaiser Health System Tracker, February 20, 2019.

This history provides both the context and background for those less familiar with the topics and helps us all more deeply understand stories like those of Jenna and her parents.

The current crisis is divided into three distinct waves, with the drugs involved in each progressive wave possessing an increase in potency, a higher risk of fatalities, and a corresponding mandate for a higher level of urgency to respond.

In the 1990s, the first wave brought the warning signs of what was to come, with a rise in prescription-related opioid overdose deaths. By 2010, the second wave hit hard, when heroin, a cheap opioid, began to flood the United States from Latin America, spiking heroin overdose deaths. Finally, in 2013, we entered the third wave of the opioid crisis with the introduction of more powerful and dangerous synthetic opioids, most notably fentanyl. This powerful drug is around a hundred times stronger than morphine, and some analogues, such as carfentanil, are approximately *ten thousand times stronger*.

Fentanyl's new popularity led to a scary watershed moment, when the odds of dying from an opioid surpassed that of motor vehicle accidents for the first time, according to the National Safety Council.[6] Fentanyl made headlines by causing the deaths of numerous public figures, including music legends Prince and Tom Petty, as well as Los Angeles Angels pitcher Tyler Skaggs and rapper Mac Miller.

While opioid misuse has driven the current sky-high addiction rates, other substances are still creating lethal outcomes. Throughout history, a societal addiction to opioids is typically followed by a societal addiction to stimulants such as amphetamine, methamphetamine, cocaine, ADHD drugs like Ritalin (aka methylphenidate), and

---

6   "Odds of Dying," NSC, accessed September 1, 2021, https://injuryfacts.nsc.org/all-injuries/preventable-death-overview/odds-of-dying/data-details/.

ritalinic acid. This is true today as well, as we are seeing a national rise in stimulant use.

If you talk to experienced health providers, they insist that alcohol is the real killer in the addiction story. Alcohol use disorder (AUD) is highly prevalent and has a significant impact on the health system due to its long-term health consequences, such as cirrhosis, hepatocellular carcinoma, and cardiovascular disease, to name a few. AUD carries a heavy cost beyond individual health issues. More than 10 percent of US children live with a parent with alcohol problems[7], while globally, alcohol misuse was the fifth leading risk factor for premature death and disability in 2010. Among people between the ages of fifteen and forty-nine, it was number one.[8] In the twenty- to thirty-nine-year-old demographic, approximately 25 percent of the total deaths were alcohol attributable. In that same year, its economic impact on the United States was $249 billion. Compared to opioids, alcohol is even easier to access and addiction to it has proven to be more common but similarly catastrophic.

These alarming statistics demonstrate the stakes are extremely high in our battle against SUD. Unfortunately, our efforts to combat this public health emergency haven't amounted to much.

Creating a New Road Map to Recovery

It is important to establish a universal approach to SUD treatment and behavioral healthcare, as we have for many major health challenges in our society. This does not mean one-size-fits-all treatment approaches. Diverse treatments are essential for the care of patients

---

7   Lisa Rapaport, "Stimulant Overdoses Rising in the US," Reuters, January 30, 2020, https://www.reuters.com/article/us-health-overdoses-stimulants/stimulant-overdoses-rising-in-the-u-s-idUSKBN1ZT367.

8   "Alcohol Use in the United States," National Institute on Alcohol Abuse and Alcoholism, June 2021, https://www.niaaa.nih.gov/publications/brochures-and-fact-sheets/alcohol-facts-and-statistics.

with addiction. However, there are some areas within traditional western medicine, such as cancer treatment, that can offer insights into standardizations of tactical strategies. For example, there are many cancer centers of excellence where treatment protocols are fairly standard. This ensures a baseline of reasonable care for individual cases.

Jill's father developed a rare type of cancer known as cholangiocarcinoma or bile duct cancer. He traveled across the US to learn of different treatment options. While one large academic center recommended the treatment, the protocol itself was carried out by a local provider. Because the protocol was fairly standardized, he could still get the appropriate care without having to travel even though he had a rare cancer.

Obviously, addiction and cancer care in many ways couldn't be more different and addiction should not and cannot be treated like cancer. But consider for a moment where there are aspects of this care delivery that could be borrowed from this example. Jill's dad had many options. In considering alternative strategies, he was able to compare options based on standardized measures of success; providers supported him in his decision-making of alternative options; aspects of the treatment were transferable across multiple states; and a strong evidence basis allowed him to determine his own unique risks and which treatment might serve him best; and lastly, care could be coordinated across multiple institutions.

We need a road map for recovery that resembles some parts of this process—where measurable outcomes and uniform definitions of success can inform tactical strategies, where standardized protocols can be implemented, where care can be coordinated across multiple institutions, and where a common language and evidence basis allow us to identify the best approach for our patients.

We will not advocate for one specific addiction remedy. Instead, we will champion a recovery road map that enables us to manage addiction as a chronic disease. SUD is not only ripe for change but also stands out as one of the most critical diseases requiring a paradigm shift. Here are some of the key reasons:

1. **Highly prevalent**—Some sources estimate upward of 22.5 million people suffer from some form of SUD. That figure continues to grow and isn't being adequately addressed.

2. **Treatment that works**—Multiple studies have identified efficacious and cost-effective therapies for OUD in particular. These studies are ineffectual if we can't supply therapies to a greater percentage of the SUD population. Current estimates suggest that only 10–20 percent of patients are in treatment.

3. **Costly acute events**—Hospital costs for SUD treatment cost billions of dollars on an annual basis. We can limit costs by implementing holistic and coordinated care methodologies over the life of the patient and avoiding costly acute events and downstream sequelae. Although difficult to achieve, the evaluation of the impact of treatment must include the total costs of care.

4. **Lack of access to care**—SUD patients receive far less treatment than those with other chronic conditions. Over 70 percent of those with depression, diabetes, and high blood pressure, for example, are receiving treatment. Fewer than 20 percent of those with SUD are.

5. **Population health management and value-based care alignment**—Through a population health approach—one

in which we address our patient populations in aggregate—
we uncover concrete opportunities to reduce crisis risks,
manage and coordinate care, and maintain patients' health.

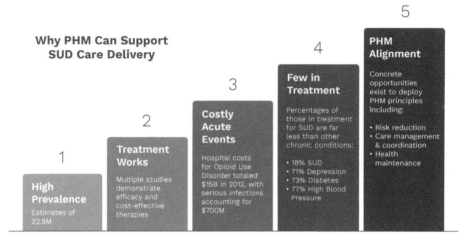

Why PHM Can Support SUD Care Delivery

1 **High Prevalence** — Estimates of 22.5M

2 **Treatment Works** — Multiple studies demonstrate efficacy and cost-effective therapies

3 **Costly Acute Events** — Hospital costs for Opioid Use Disorder totaled $15B in 2012, with serious infections accounting for $700M

4 **Few in Treatment** — Percentages of those in treatment for SUD are far less than other chronic conditions:
• 18% SUD
• 71% Depression
• 73% Diabetes
• 77% High Blood Pressure

5 **PHM Alignment** — Concrete opportunities exist to deploy PHM principles including:
• Risk reduction
• Care management & coordination
• Health maintenance

Source: Crowley R et al., 2017. Annals Int Med 166:10, 733-736

If our healthcare ecosystem is successful at creating this kind of
road map, the following benefits will be realized:

- **Lives will be saved.** Families will be rebuilt and reconnected;
  communities will have balance restored; and health providers
  will be empowered to achieve their goals of better outcomes
  and a higher level of care in the SUD space.

- **Money will be used more efficiently.** Government agencies
  and healthcare institutions will provide more bang for the
  buck, reducing the cost of care for taxpayers and organizations.

- **Quality of life will improve.** People suffering from SUD
  will become active members of their families and communities, contribute to the economy, and be able to live full,
  productive lives. Even if they continue to live with addiction,
  they will be able to mitigate and/or forestall the disease's
  downstream effects.

- **Health institutions and caregivers will enjoy a higher success rate.** With a unifying and disruptive programmatic strategy for tackling this crisis in place, protocols will empower more positive outcomes for patients.

- **Private investment will promote improvements in care and reap the benefits of success.** When private money enters this field, there will be financial pressure to succeed, promoting innovation and improvements in outcomes. One can't argue that cancer care isn't big business, and with that we've seen an exponential acceleration in outcomes. It's time for SUD to enjoy the benefit.

These are lofty ambitions, but they are attainable. Often, the secret to success for meeting an overwhelming challenge begins with having the right mindset. We must change the way we think about treating addiction. Before we can change the way we think about treating addiction, we need to change the way that we think about addiction itself. As first introduced by Robert Granfield and William Cloud in *Coming Clean: Overcoming Addiction without Treatment*, we are addressing the recovery capital for our patients, recognizing that success for our patients is a combination of both internal factors and external resources. While there are an extensive number of available resources for patients with SUD, the overall effectiveness of these resources hinges on the ability of our patients to access them and leverage them to good effect and the ability to coordinate care across these disparate sources. Let's return to the story of Jenna's parents, Greg and Dawn, the story we opened this chapter with. It's an inspiring example of how the change we're talking about can happen with the smallest steps.

Jenna had called the last time and said, "Mom, there's this girl named Paige. And she really, really wants to get better. And I know she can do it, but her parents have no money. Would you just send money for her for a couple of weeks in sober living? And I know she can make it." And I said to her, "Jenna, we can't help everybody." And she answered, "Mom, I'm going to commit myself to eight months, nine months in here. When I get out, you and I are a team. We're going to raise money. And we're going to help people that don't have the resources to get into treatment and sober living and save lives and educate people about this."

And that's why we started our foundation, Jenna's Promise. What Jenna's Promise is doing is building people. We sponsor people financially to get from inpatient or incarceration into sober living. We received a grant from ADAP (Vermont's federally funded, state-run department of Alcohol and Drug Abuse Prevention), but we've also spent about $30,000 of our own money helping these people. Some of them fail again, but our percentages are a lot higher than the norm. We're building people and some of them are going to make it the first time, some of them might come through two or three times, but each person we build or help, we actually give the opportunity to build themselves. We're just there to help build.

Now, through her life insurance money, Jenna is going to help hundreds of people, maybe thousands over a long time period. So, we lost her, but she's not gone. She's helping people as we speak.

By effectively coordinating care, leveraging financial resources effectively, and creating a more intentionally woven web to support our patients, our systems will be transformed to better guide SUD patients to recovery.

In the next chapter, let's explore what needs to change.

CHAPTER TWO

ADDICTION: PERCEPTION VERSUS REALITY

There is nothing either good or bad but thinking makes it so.

—WILLIAM SHAKESPEARE

How we view a problem can either empower a strong solution—or work against it.

Our perspective particularly applies to the prism through which we view addiction. We'll explore this idea further, but first, let's unpack the current state of treatment. In a landscape fraught with holes, access to addiction treatment is improving. Short-term treatment is increasingly accessible for most, with state monies to fund detoxification and transitional care. Recent advances in some states have enabled this care to be initiated immediately following an overdose in the ED. Unfortunately, if not effectively transitioned into care, most individuals will return to the ED.

Addiction requires a long-term strategy to effectively care for patients. Right now, patients may only receive crisis care, or isolated treatments for potentially dangerous circumstances. It is vitally important that crisis care is readily available. In fact, the federal government has put together substantial resources to support appropriate crisis-care management, as best described in the National Guidelines for Behavioral Health Crisis Care Best Practice Toolkit (2020).

For the rare individual, a trip to the ED may actually be the impetus for change. For most, however, crisis care simply begets more crisis care and more cost. Patients in the ED may be well known to providers and labeled as "frequent flyers." As highlighted by Soril et al., approximately 1–5 percent of ED patients account for 12–18 percent of ED visits.[9] While there is some debate as to whether ED access is a result of misuse of resources for nonurgent care needs versus incorrectly managed upstream social and chronic health issues, we can all agree that this revolving door of care does not benefit our hospital systems, provider resources, or most importantly, our patients.

At present, 70–85 percent of people who only receive crisis care will relapse within the first twelve months of recovery. Those relapses frequently bring them right back into EDs, with an associated risk of overdose fatality, tragic losses of life that might have been preventable with better long-term treatment strategies. Further, this way of using clinical resources places a high-cost burden on the system, overloads ED staff, promotes provider burnout, and does not address the long-term care needs of our patients.

If, as part of crisis care, individuals are engaged in some form of detoxification but leave without a secure step down, they are more

---

9   Lesley J. J. Soril et al., "Reducing Frequent Visits to the Emergency Department: A Systematic Review of Interventions," *PLoS One*, 2015.

vulnerable to further overdoses since detoxification lowers their tolerance for the drug. Resumed use after detoxification at the same level can trigger overdose.

When Dr. Sharif Nankoe was a medical resident in the ED, he experienced the impact of the SUD epidemic on the hospital system.

> Patients who end up in the ED are often there due to overdose … I saw patients repeatedly showing up with overdoses. Some would leave before you even finished monitoring them. You treat them with Narcan and you want to observe them for a few hours to make sure, because the Narcan only works for a short amount of time. You want to make sure that once it wears off the patient is awake and alert because if they took a long-acting opioid, like methadone, for example, then that outlasts the Narcan and the overdose is going to resume.
>
> A good number of patients would just leave before you've even had the chance to fully evaluate them. I saw patients die—plenty of patients with opioid related complications—whether it's an abscess or endocarditis or a spinal abscess or other complications. And it's not just opioids. The number of patients with alcohol intoxication or withdrawal, or alcohol and opioid related complications … it's just a huge part of emergency medicine.

The human toll of this loop of recovery and relapse can be staggering—as it is to the cost to our health system. In New York City alone, opioid patients accounted for forty-five thousand emergency room visits in 2017, creating huge pressure on an already financially-strapped healthcare system.[10] According to a 2011 study in the *American Journal of Pharmacy Benefits*, patients with untreated SUD tend to incur $18,000 more in annual healthcare costs than those without SUD. A patient with SUD will typically experience more deteriorating effects with each ED visit, requiring a higher level of treatment and longer stays. The current opioid epidemic continues to exacerbate the financial pressure on healthcare facilities in a volatile, ever-changing healthcare ecosystem.

RISING COSTS

A study from Boston's Beth Israel Deaconess Medical Center found that the average cost of treating an opioid overdose victim in intensive care units jumped 58 percent between 2009 and 2020.

Episodes of nonadherence to treatment occur in virtually all chronic medical conditions, such as asthma and hypertension. Treatments for these types of diseases can require changing deeply rooted behaviors, which is often an extremely difficult proposition. Ask anyone who's tried to diet, commit to a New Year's resolution, or otherwise change ingrained unhealthy habits—it requires a level of discipline that not everyone can muster.

However, there are some significant differences when it comes to relapses. First, the stigma of having SUD, which we'll explore further, creates barriers to treatment access. Second, these types of pharmacological agents hijack the patient's brain in a very profound

---

10   Corinne Ramey, "NYC: Opioid Crisis Has Cost City $500 Million," *The Wall Street Journal*, February 26, 2018, https://www.wsj.com/articles/nyc-opioid-crisis-has-cost-city-500-million-1519682333?reflink=desktopwebshare_permalink.

way, causing extensive rewiring to such an extent that the patient can lose control of their own decision-making. Third, while all chronic diseases carry short-term risks associated with treatment failures, such as diabetic ketoacidosis or acute asthma exacerbations, those related to SUD overdoses may be even more devastating and rapid.

We can and should do better. We must combine our understanding of the unique aspects of SUD with some core principles of how to manage chronic disease.

With the right long-term treatment approach in place, we can meet the following goals:

- Many crises can be prevented from happening in the first place. If they do occur, protocols would limit them from recurring.

- Local mental health, community, and outpatient-based treatment organizations can work to mitigate referrals to inpatient and ED settings by optimizing outpatient management and coordinating care when referrals are necessary.

- Discharges from the emergency department and inpatient settings can support warm handoffs with active transitions to long-term care solutions.

- The healthcare system in general can save money, reduce costly acute events, and improve margins with this type of long-term care. Providers will finally have clear-cut paths of treatment for those suffering from SUD, supporting their complex care needs.

This isn't pie-in-the-sky thinking: these objectives have, in a fragmented way, been achieved in some places. Nonetheless, one of the biggest blockades in the way of attaining these goals is *the public perception of the addiction.* The stigma associated with addiction needs to change before we can make substantial progress.

The Stigma of Addiction

Despite addiction finally being classified as a disease in 1987, our cultural view of it hasn't evolved nearly as much as it should have since that official designation. Too many still view addiction as a sign of personal weakness or moral failing rather than a chronic condition.

> The stigma associated with addiction needs to change before we can make substantial progress.

The battle against the opioid crisis is sometimes called a "silent war." The impact of stigma is debilitating. Those with SUD may be unwilling to admit addictions, let alone seek treatment for them, because of the societal shame. The family and friends of these patients may play right into that cycle of shame and enable the disease to continue untreated. An expert in the field of addiction, Sharon Wegscheider-Cruse, has highlighted how addiction can become a disease of the family and has characterized six personae that individual family members can play in the disease process: the addicted, the hero, the enabler, the mascot, the scapegoat, and the lost child. For additional information on the role of family, please refer to the resource section at the end of the book.

Researchers recognize five different types of stigmas that each affect our ability to treat patients: public, courtesy, structural, self, and multiple stigma. While nuanced, we must recognize that there are multiple forces at play when managing patients.

Five Types of Stigma

Types of Stigma	Description
Public Stigma	Societal discrimination toward a group of people
Courtesy Stigma	Discrimination or prejudice against individuals supporting those individuals (e.g. family, providers)
Structural Stigma	Organizational policies or actions that limit the group's opportunities
Self-Stigma	An individual within the group internalizes public perceptions
Multiple Stigma	The synergistic effect of being part of more than one stigmatized group

Dr. Nankoe explains how the stigma of SUD is "baked in the cake" of even the medical community:

If you're a substance use disorder patient coming into the ED, oh my God! So much stigma and judgment, it starts right there. It's not like people overtly display it, but certainly, when patients come into the ED, one of the first things that crosses the mind [of] the staff is that this person is looking to get a prescription for opioids. That is very prevalent and absolutely common. Even when I talk to my patients in the community about their ER experiences, the shaming they experienced is still very much there.

You have to do a whole culture change and that's going to take some time ... and reinforcement. It's not just about giving people one training and then expecting them to change. It's just going to take time and lots of exposure to the concept that this is a chronic brain disease.

Think about it: When we find out someone has cancer or diabetes, it's not hard to feel empathy for the person. These are regarded as "real" diseases that, for the most part, are beyond the patient's control. By contrast, when we hear someone labeled as a "junkie," a "pill popper," a "drunk," or one of many other derogatory terms, it may be hard not to jump to a negative conclusion about them. That's why so many conceal their addictions—or do their best to try—because it's regarded as a mark of shame and a moral failing. That harsh judgment can trigger more behavioral health issues that can worsen an already-existing addiction problem.

Antistigma Material

Stigmatized Language	Non-Stigmatized Language
Addict; User; Drug Abuser; Junkie; Substance Abuser	Person With a Substance Use Disorder; Person Who Uses Drugs; Person Who Misuses Medication
Former Addict; Saying Someone is "Clean"	Person in Recovery; Person Who is Abstinent
Dirty or Clean Drug Test	Positive or Negative Test Results
Opioid Replacement (Treatment)	Medication for Opioid Use Disorder
IV Drug Abuser or User	Person Who Injects Drugs
Alcoholic	Person With Alcohol Use Disorder

This stigma reaches into other vital areas of our society—even into the healthcare system that's supposed to help patients. Consider that when it comes to the opioid crisis, we make it far easier for patients to obtain the source of the problem rather than a solution. There are roughly nine hundred thousand physicians in America, and pretty much all of them are able to prescribe OxyContin, Percocet, or any other opioid-based pain medicine. However, while rules are ever changing, only approximately one in ten primary care providers are certified to prescribe buprenorphine—a critical medication for medication-assisted treatment (MAT) for opioid addiction.

In addition, a common misperception by some medical offices in upscale areas is that providers may prefer not to handle addiction cases, because they perceive those particular patients as being at best downscale and at worst dangerous. As highlighted at the 2019 Hope Conference by Dr. Kelly Ramsey, providers may say, "I don't want those patients in my waiting room (or pharmacy ...)" or "The flood-gates will open." Attempts to address stigma may be exacerbated by the strategic placement of some public facilities to improve access as being regarded as on the wrong side of the tracks. These misconceptions may serve to further perpetuate stigma and should be addressed head on within our healthcare organizations.

Perhaps the most severe stigma has been placed on addiction by our justice system. Arrests of those in possession of drugs have routinely resulted in harsh jail sentences. The Human Rights Watch organization has documented the challenges of those who fall into this quagmire. According to one Human Rights Watch report, one convict, who suffered from a rare autoimmune disease, served at least five years in prison for possessing a small amount of cocaine and a crack pipe and feared he wouldn't survive his sentence. Another woman, incarcerated for having a baggie that contained only heroin residue, lost her student financial aid, some promising career opportunities, and even the food stamps she used to feed her three kids.

In the words of one of these victims of excessive sentencing, "Do they realize what they are doing to people's lives in here? Because of my drug addiction, they just keep punishing me ... I have been to prison five times, and it's destroyed me."[11]

---

11   "US: Disastrous Toll of Criminalizing Drug Use," Human Rights Watch, October 12, 2016, https://www.hrw.org/news/2016/10/12/us-disastrous-toll-criminalizing-drug-use#.

By treating addiction like a crime rather than an illness, policies unfortunately fed the stigma rather than minimized it. They also impeded care and recovery—it's harder to get access to proper SUD care in prison. And once an SUD patient was released, their road to recovery was infinitely more difficult because they had to deal with the additional stigmas that came with being labeled an ex-con. If anything, the support they received from society at large was even less than they'd had before they went to jail—increasing the odds of these patients relapsing and ending up in the ED ... or even back behind bars.

Today policymakers are rethinking the so-called War on Drugs as they struggle to cope with both the explosion in prison population and the destruction of communities in the wake of overwhelming addiction. Most justice policy experts recommend treatment over the harsh prison sentences of the past. However, unless and until treatment improves, many patients will find themselves shuttled between the ED and prison as the limited resources available to them fail and they turn to illegal means to support their escalating habits.

TRANSFORMING THE WAR ON DRUGS

The war on drugs, drugs won. We lost. But there's so much progress that can come from that. There's so much more money that can be allocated toward treatment. Also, you're changing the trajectory of individuals' lives, who are struggling with the disease. This isn't a behavior issue. You have a disease that influences behavior, not the other way around.

—Cam Lauf, Executive Director, Turning Point Center, Burlington, Vermont

Most importantly, when the justice system brands you as a criminal for your drug use, the stigma grows by leaps and bounds. People can become even more reluctant to discuss their addiction problem or seek treatment. In the past few years, the justice system and imprisonment have made substantial progress in SUD care in prison and at release. Importantly, there has been remarkable avoidance of incarceration through treatment courts; however, the stigma connected to jail time and SUD still lingers.

The Link between Behavioral Health and Addiction

We mentioned how diseases like cancer and diabetes aren't stigmatized like addiction is. These two chronic conditions generally require a lifetime of management, just like addiction, and the medical community works hard to provide that long-term care. However, a patient with SUD is managed differently.

An author of this book, Chris Powell, knows personally how these differences play out. Chris's father was an alcoholic who attempted to reassure his family he had it under control. He went to Alcoholics Anonymous meetings and other support groups and would come back to the house vowing that he was done with drinking. He promised the family he was finished with that kind of self-destructive behavior.

Then he did it over and over again.

He didn't drink every day, but maybe once a week he would just never come home from work. Chris was able to know, based solely on what his father wore when he left in the morning, just when that was going to happen. Come early afternoon, his dad was suddenly impossible to reach because he would have already gone to hit the bars, where he would shoot pool and drink heavily. When he came home, he instigated physical abuse of Chris's mother.

On some of those nights when he didn't come home, Chris's mother would put him and his brother in the car and drive from bar to bar in different towns looking for him. The brothers would wait nervously in the back of the car while she went into every watering hole she happened on and tried to find him.

The brothers didn't actually want her to succeed in her quest—because things quickly spiraled out of control when she did. As she pulled their father out of the bar, they would both be screaming at each other, pushing each other around, and doing other assorted bad things that children should never see. (This vicious cycle started when Chris was around six years old and continued well into his early teens.)

His father would promise the next day that he wasn't going to do it anymore. But, like many others, he couldn't shake his addiction on his own and there wasn't any place to turn to other than AA meetings, because the stigma was so prevalent.

Chris's father's regret seemed real. His commitment to overcoming his alcoholism seemed genuine. Yet his relapsing was a constant. Was he a weak man because he couldn't control his alcohol intake? Was he a lesser man? No. He couldn't do it, because he was in the grips of a chronic disease. But it wasn't seen that way. The result? Nobody's going to try and cure a disease that no one categorizes as a disease.

We know so much more about addiction today, and we've uncovered many substantive links to related mental health conditions. Multiple studies have shown that many who experience a mental illness during their lives will also develop SUD—and vice versa. Over 60 percent of adolescents in community-based treatment programs meet the criteria for mental illness. Data shows high rates of comorbid SUDs and anxiety disorders as well as ADHD, depression, bipolar disorder, antisocial personality disorders, etc. Patients with schizophrenia also experience higher rates of SUD than the general population.

Co-Occurrence of SUD & Behavioral Health

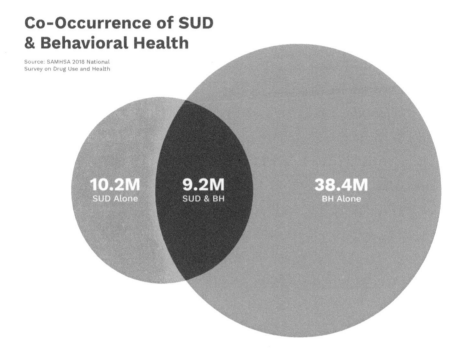

Source: SAMHSA 2018 National Survey on Drug Use and Health

10.2M
SUD Alone

9.2M
SUD & BH

38.4M
BH Alone

Statistics can only tell us so much; the biological underpinnings are also very compelling. Repeated studies have demonstrated that addiction is a product of our brain's wiring. While other diseases such as Alzheimer's and brain tumors cause a great deal of easily seen damage in the brain, the damage to someone with SUD experiences can be more subtle. Recognizing it was a fallacy to suggest drug and alcohol dependency was largely mental or a failure of willpower, many scientists, including neurologist Christian Lüscher and National Institute on Drug Abuse (NIDA) director Nora Volkow, demonstrated that addiction didn't kill neurons in the brain—instead, it somehow rewired their connections in a maladaptive way.[12]

Physiological addiction to drugs and alcohol alters brain chemistry, resulting in impaired judgment and decision making. Those biochemical changes incorporate a warped form of learning and implant it into the most primitive areas of the brain due to the effects of dopamine, the so-called pleasure chemical. The brain becomes focused on feeding itself with a dopamine surge. Nothing remains as important as feeding that dopamine influx. The damaged brain and compromised decision-making create destabilization in foundational ways. Housing, maintaining a job, caring for children, or abiding by the law are no longer as important as feeding the brain with the drug.

The truth about dopamine is more complicated than that— the chemical is actually more about motivating us toward certain behaviors that we believe will bring us some sort of reward. Nonetheless, the reliance on dopamine release hijacks the individual's central ability to make decisions and, in the words of the head of NIDA, Nora Volkow, "compromises a person's free will."

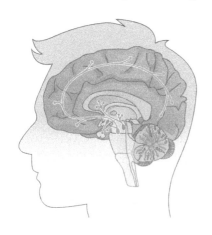

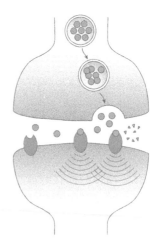

Dopamine Pathways in the Brain

Release of Dopamine Neurotransmitters at the Level of the Neuron

12   Adam Piore, "Resetting the Addictive Brain," *Discover*, April 1, 2015, https://www.discovermaga-zine.com/mind/resetting-the-addictive-brain.

Many addictive drugs increase dopamine release or block its reuptake into neurons following release. Even though the addictive behavior brings about unwelcome outcomes, the rewired neurons create a memory that's actually pleasant ... which prompts the person with SUD to reengage in destructive old habits and lose interest in behaviors that actually do bring them natural rewards. It also causes a spike in craving the substance, which is the basis of the SUD, even after a long period of abstinence. As the withdrawal period lengthens, the craving becomes stronger rather than weaker, which is why relapses are so common.

How Our Healthcare System Sidesteps Effective SUD Treatment

While SUD can be categorized as a behavioral health issue, it's still a challenge to get proper BH treatment within our existing health system. The National Alliance on Mental Illness reports that 25 percent of Americans experience a mental illness incident each year.

The fact is, however, BH has always gotten short shrift. A 2018 survey from the National Council for Behavioral Health shows that 56 percent of patients faced significant obstacles to getting treatment. Limitations in health insurance have historically been a substantial contributing factor. Many of these limitations have been surmounted by efforts associated with the Mental Health Parity and Addiction Equity Act; however, we now are in the midst

> The fact is, however, BH has always gotten short shrift.

of an alarming mental health clinician shortage that cuts across all 50 states, according to the Kaiser Family Foundation (KFF). These shortages can result in long-distance travel to find the right provider, if one can be found at all. While the COVID-19 pandemic has accelerated telehealth services, enabling increased access to mental health services, a number of patients remain untreated in the face of provider shortages.

While treatment centers provide a supportive and welcoming point of entry for many patients, individuals often must rely on several organizations on their journey to recovery. Further, we collectively still struggle to determine what constitutes success among the various providers. Attempts to derive reliable measures of outcomes are hindered by the lack of publicly available data sets and independent verification of success. Even AA, which has been in existence for decades, doesn't release data on its members' success rate.

"What we have in this country is a washing-machine model of addiction treatment," says A. Thomas McLellan, chief executive of the nonprofit Treatment Research Institute, based in Philadelphia. "You go to Shady Acres for 30 days, or to some clinic for 60 visits or 60 doses, whatever it is. And then you're discharged and everyone's crying and hugging and feeling proud—and you're supposed to be cured … It doesn't really matter if you're a movie star going to some resort by the sea or a homeless person. The system doesn't work well for what for many people is a chronic, recurring problem."[13]

Once we accept that addiction is indeed a chronic disease, it's easy to see just how insufficient our current system of treatment is. Imagine a patient with diabetes only receiving crisis care—having a limb amputated and sent on their way. Absurd, right? It's no less absurd to send an overdose patient back home after they're stabilized and not expect further and more severe health consequences down the line.

---

13   Benedict Carey, "Drug Rehabilitation or Revolving Door?" *New York Times*, December 22, 2008, https://www.nytimes.com/2008/12/23/health/23reha.html.

We need a sea change in our perception of addiction treatment. The closest example to what could be accomplished with such a change occurred during the AIDS/HIV epidemic, which began in the early 1980s.

STIGMA AND CHRONIC DISEASE

I think the biggest reason people fall out of treatment prematurely, I suspect, is stigma, and just the incredible challenges we force people to add to their lives if they want to stay in treatment. We don't treat it like other chronic diseases.

—Miro Weinberger, Mayor, Burlington, Vermont

When cases first started cropping up, HIV also suffered from being stigmatized because mostly gay men and drug users were being infected—so HIV was considered a "dirty" disease that strictly impacted societal outliers. Many a preacher stepped up to their pulpit and declared AIDS was God's punishment for sinful behavior, and too many bought into that line of thinking. Even though people were dying, the disease was largely relegated to the shadows.

Celebrity influence gave the disease more prominence in national discourse: actor Rock Hudson announced he had AIDS. Hudson, who passed away shortly after disclosure of the disease, had been a personal friend of President Ronald Reagan—who, according to numerous accounts (including an April 2021 *Atlantic* article), exhibited a longstanding "unwillingness to recognize and confront the AIDS epidemic … one of the deepest and most enduring scars on its legacy."

Even Dr. Anthony Fauci, the infectious disease expert who has been an integral part of the management of the COVID-19 pandemic, found himself confronting his own stigmatization of AIDS. Although he was one of the first in the scientific community to take HIV seriously (and was labeled an "alarmist" for his efforts), he stuck to the FDA's cumbersome and inflexible drug-approval process to discover a treatment, despite the escalating number of victims who were dying of the disease. Real progress was so slow that protestors surrounded the National Institutes of Health in Bethesda, Maryland, where Fauci had his office. "God, I hated him," said Larry Kramer, a prominent writer and activist. "As far as I was concerned, he was the central focus of evil in the world."[14]

When the gay community unleashed its full fury, most bureaucrats reacted to the protestors' look and lifestyle rather than what they were trying to communicate. On that score, Fauci decided to challenge his own prejudice. "Let me put aside the goth dress—the earrings and the Mohawk haircuts and the black jackets—and just listen to what they have to say. And what they were saying made absolutely perfect sense." Fauci reversed himself and decided to become a public health activist who happened to be a federal government employee. He built strong relationships within the gay community, earned their confidence and respect, and ended up speeding up drug trials in order to find effective treatments as quickly as possible.

As a result of his and others' efforts, urgency increased toward finding effective HIV treatment protocols. The result was the disease gradually ceased to be a death sentence. The development of valid treatments to care for HIV patients removed some of the fear associated with the disease and converted it from a deadly disease of

---

14   Michael Specter, "How Anthony Fauci Became America's Doctor," *New Yorker*, April 20, 2020, https://www.newyorker.com/magazine/2020/04/20/how-anthony-fauci-became-americas-doctor.

unknown origins into a manageable chronic disease. Those with HIV know it will remain a lifelong health issue. They know their mindset has to be, "Yeah, I have HIV, and I have to manage it for the rest of my life." Today, that's not a difficult ask. Treatment is more accessible than ever and takes a holistic approach that also addresses HIV comorbidities, essential to a patient's ongoing health.

This is *exactly* the level of treatment addiction needs to be elevated to—as a lifelong chronic disease that must be managed, not as a moral failing on the part of those struggling with it. Someone should be able to say, "Yes, I am in long-term recovery now and have been sober for two years." Ideally, the individual can identify supports in place to manage the long-term needs.

Once addiction is finally perceived as a chronic disease—not unlike HIV, diabetes, or cancer—we can finally establish and implement holistic programmatic approaches for long-term treatment, which will result in improved care and reduced volumes and margins. Medical professionals like Dr. Nankoe are already creating positive change with their open-minded approaches.

I grew up in a family where our family really cared about social justice and poverty alleviation and that's always been at my core. This is a vastly underserved population. I saw that in the ED and I saw that also in primary care practice. Some of my colleagues were not as eager to treat these patients, but I wanted to—so, after residency, I focused on treatment of SUD in the community, and within seven months or so after residency, I actually became the Medical Director of the Opioid Treatment Program at two of Vermont's hubs, as we call them. A little over a year later, the Vermont correctional system's healthcare contractor asked me to help out with their correctional MAT program as a consultant, and then eventually asked me to take it over from the medical side. That's what I'm sticking with. That's really where I feel at home.

In the next chapter, we'll reveal what we believe are the necessary first steps to providing support to the many, many SUD patients who aren't getting the help they need to recover.

CHAPTER THREE

THE WHOLE PERSON BEHIND THE PATIENT

If you are broken, you do not have to stay broken.

—SELENA GOMEZ

Recovery from SUD is like a marathon.

While there are some obvious differences, there are some interesting parallels worth exploring. In both cases, the goal isn't necessarily how you get to the finish line or how much time it takes to reach it. For a lot of people, success is simply about getting through. It's about surviving the process and saying, "I did it." That process—and the support systems that keep it in place—is essential to the person reaching their goal. You can't just go out and run a marathon—or at least very few of us can. Most people would fail miserably if they walked out the door one day with no training and no support systems and attempted to run twenty-six miles. While anyone can certainly go out and train on their own, there are nearly endless resources available to support them if they need some help. Dozens of books offer everything from training methods to dietary advice to what author Mackenzie L. Havey's *The Perfect Run* calls "cultivating a near-effortless running state." There are also online communities to turn to for advice and motivation, personal trainers, and coaches to help design and oversee their race plan and on and on and on.

This system of supports enables a person to enter a race with a detailed, personalized plan designed to help them get through it, with instructions ranging from the pace they should maintain to how to deal with the specific setbacks they're likely to face. Simply by following the plan, the runner can avoid the rookie mistakes that derail most newbies, like starting too fast and winding up spent with twenty more miles to go. They're far more likely to get through it and make it to the end.

Even once the race starts, the marathon runner still isn't left on their own. The course is clearly marked and free of obstacles. Mile markers keep them aware of how far they've come and how far they have left to go. Every few miles, there's an aid station where they can hydrate and take some gel goo and eat a banana or an apple because they're burning calories and they need to be replenished. There's even a medical team ready to come to their rescue should anything go wrong.

All these supports work together to serve one purpose—to help the runner achieve their goal.

When SUD recovery is the goal, however, there is no finish line. "Getting through it" simply means staying in a race they will need to run every day of their life, for the rest of their life. And while we've all heard stories of people who have successfully gone cold turkey, kicked addiction, and solved their underlying behavioral health issues on their own, statistically, there aren't very many of them.

According to the National Center for Biotechnology Information (NCBI), "Relapse rate after opioid detoxification ranges from

72 to 88% after 12–36 months, despite multidisciplinary endeavors, though a six-month controlled study has shown lower relapse rate (32–70%)."[15] Just like marathon runners, people in recovery from SUD need support to achieve their goal. The difference is that they need it from providers, family, and friends—and they will need it for a lifetime.

SUD patients also need a plan to deal with the setbacks they're likely to face over the course of their marathon. They need solid strategies in place to help them cope with the inevitable ups and downs and occasional surprises without relapsing. Most importantly, they need a supportive community—including engaged community resources; mechanisms to connect back into care or call for help; social connection; nonjudgment; and ready access to housing, employment, food, skill development, educational opportunities, and childcare—to rely on when things get hard. Because they invariably will.

Cancer, HIV, and diabetes are similarly difficult conditions to manage, and patients with those diseases are increasingly receiving the kind of coordinated, whole-patient care that will help them get through it and manage their conditions.

But when a patient with SUD enters the system, it may look more like this …

In any encounter with law enforcement, medical professionals or emergency medical professionals, there was never a conversation about my substance use. But let's not forget. I'm a privileged white kid. Every time I got pulled over, I wasn't scared for my life.... I was like, "All right, I'm going to spend the night in jail and that's it. I'll get off." That

---

15   Harsh Chalana, Tanu Kundal, Varun Gupta, Amandeep Singh Malhari, "Predictors of Relapse after Inpatient Opioid Detoxification during 1-Year Follow-Up," *Journal of Addiction*, 2016, https://doi.org/10.1155/2016/7620860.

privilege weighed heavily on how I would respond to these consequences.

During the time from my freshman year in high school to senior year, I had been arrested I think three times. I had wrecked two cars. I had various fines from the great city of Baltimore, Maryland. I had near-death experiences, almost crashing my car, because I loved drinking and driving.

One time when I was eighteen, I blacked out and was found on the side of the street in a nicer part of Baltimore City. I woke up at Johns Hopkins Emergency Department, in a hospital bed. They had my information because I had an ID and a health insurance card in my wallet. And I woke up, ripped the IVs out and just walked right out of the hospital.

I had used, I had snorted and injected heroin, however, I never fully had a physical dependence until I started to snort Suboxone, which was readily available and much stronger than the synthetic opioids that were being produced for painkillers. Suddenly here's this new therapeutic drug that's used for treatment, but also not being regulated at the rate that it should. It was just flooding the streets, and it was also an opiate. Once I shot up heroin for the first time, it was "Oh my God, that's it." It's this amazing euphoria that you've never experienced in your entire life. And it happens once. And then … after you do it, that's it. You need to find that every single time, because nothing else matters, nothing comes close enough to it.

I overdosed three times, none of which sent me to the emergency department thanks to a quick-thinking friend, who was able to reverse them. The only time I went to the emergency department for heroin was after my mother went in the bathroom and started screaming because she found my stash. She forced me to go to the emergency department. We went and checked in, and I started to withdraw because I hadn't had any substances. And they did a lot of discussion with my mom and nothing with me. It put all the responsibility on her.

The next two and a half years was a battle of me in and out of treatment programs, in and out of jail, in and out of sober housing and homelessness. Finally, I moved to Vermont from Maryland. There, I began medication assisted treatment. I started to use Suboxone, but the treatment did not work for me because I didn't have any skin in the game. I wasn't making a conscious effort to dedicate my life to recovery. I was really just half-assing it to get the restraints off.

… They [the providers] did their job. They did what was medically recommended, what was the best science at the time and what was common practice. My mom did everything by the book. But I wasn't willing to help myself. There needs to be a partnership, right?

You can't just pick somebody up and force them to do something. I mean, look at criminal reform, look at incarceration. What has that done to changing individuals when recidivism rates are through the roof?

—Cam Lauf, Executive Director, Turning Point Center, Burlington, Vermont

As Cam said, you can't force a person into recovery. You have to meet them where they're at. If and/or when they're ready, we need to be ready as well. We need to have a support structure in place that will help them get through (and remain in) the process. Otherwise, they'll get lost in a system that isn't designed to support or help anyone. That will leave them likely to wind up back in the ED, and the whole tragic cycle will start over again.

> You can't force a person into recovery. You have to meet them where they're at.

Unfortunately, that's what happens all too often—because we don't have the proper support structure in place for those with SUD. Our system's current approach to treatment doesn't allow for that. Let's dig deeper into these care gaps.

What We're Doing Isn't Working

While addiction is a chronic illness that requires long-term treatment like diabetes or hypertension, our current approach to SUD treatment still relies heavily upon acute, episodic care with minimal cross-institutional or cross-departmental coordination. The overreliance on crisis care has accelerated financial costs and the loss of life. Every social and economic stratum in our country has felt the impact. For the past two years, the average life expectancy of Americans has declined specifically because of SUD, not only affecting patients but also spreading that tragedy to their parents, spouses, children, friends, and beyond their immediate circle and out into their communities. While we have made substantial strides in improving the accessibility of MAT treatment, developed pockets of community engagement across the country, and in some locations, built an infrastructure to support care, we continue to struggle to stem this tragic tide.

FEDERAL COORDINATION

There is substantial need for improved coordination of grant programs at the federal level, particularly with the aid of the White House Office of National Drug Control Policy. Enhanced federal coordination of opioid funding programs across federal agencies will improve program coordination at the state level. This is critical given the sheer volume of grants going to states, the need for coordination across state agencies and local governments, and the multifaceted nature of the epidemic.

—Bipartisan Policy Center

Our federal and state governments—and by extension, taxpayers—have continued to supply needed grant funding and support for treatment programs. But at least so far, all that funding isn't making a sufficient dent in the problem—largely because of how it's being spent. The Bipartisan Policy Center took an objective look at how federal funding was targeted to take on the opioid crisis and discovered resources were being spent on a myriad of programs without much thought as to how they might work together to provide more effective outcomes.

However, this type of coordination has yet to take place, in funding or in SUD care writ large. Healthcare institutions likewise throw money at the problem but continue to miss the mark. Business investment into SUD and behavioral health will return better outcomes. As mentioned previously, other chronic diseases have a large body of work completed by private enterprises that supplement grant-funded efforts. This private sector investment will enable the ability to scale, converting what is often one-off grant work to have a broad-scale impact. Private investment in improving care should not be looked at with distrust but opportunity for significant advancement in the fight for long-term recovery for every patient.

Instead, the real-time responsibility for managing this crisis has fallen to providers. As a result, EDs are overwhelmed. Often hospital beds are occupied by overdose patients. Sadly, providers are not equipped to give these patients the deep-level care they really need. Providers only have so much bandwidth and training and so many tools. The medical and social complexities experienced by many of these individuals can hardly be attended to in one outpatient visit. As a result, these complexities are often overlooked, and the patient is shuttled through the system.

Why does SUD care remain so fragmented? The medical community has more than enough expertise to tackle addiction head on. It also has the money, an avalanche of research, and an overabundance of scientific talent necessary to innovate new strategies that will provide more sustainable relief to patients and providers alike.

Yet we still *don't* have a unified strategy at the institutional level to deal with this ongoing crisis. Without it, all the various branches of healthcare remain divided in their approaches, each dealing as best as they can with individual patients, each bearing the burden of this crisis alone.

In the past few years, the emphasis has been on ending the overprescribing of opioids, and there are solid reasons for this focus on this front end of the addiction loop—both to avoid the most immediate threat to patients' health and to avoid liability (e.g., Purdue Pharma is currently paying out ten to twelve billion dollars to settle claims). However, consider that maybe a real motivator is that the prescription part of the process is the easiest to control. Cut off the supply and the person with an SUD has no choice but to change their ways, right? Unfortunately, as we've discussed, the rewired brain of a person with SUD coupled with often complex physical and social care needs gets overlooked in this approach. This can lead to the patient receiving care that may not be optimized for their needs

There has been some material progress in this area. In the past, an overdose victim would receive a Narcan reversal and then be sent home. Over the past twenty years of this crisis, we've evolved to the point where ED staff may now provide, in addition to Narcan, a two-to-four-day prescription for buprenorphine, which treats pain as well as narcotic addiction. While this "soft handoff" is a slight improvement, a few pills don't take the place of a true warm handoff, which would involve a referral to a medical professional who can lay out a proper path for recovery and, in an ideal world, serve as the patient's conduit to a supportive, coordinated care team with a holistic approach to patient care.

Additionally, while larger health systems are beginning to create at least the basics of that kind of recovery network for patients, many Americans receive care in rural health settings, where robust, ongoing care programs may be difficult to access. Initiatives to support rural care require extensive commitments to telehealth, transportation, and professional training for local providers.

While the American Society of Addiction Medicine developed placement criteria decades ago, patients are often at a higher acuity by the time they reach care. This can translate to the delivery of care in very high-cost settings. As patients are introduced into care with arguably escalated physical and mental health requirements, they can become very complex to manage. Treatment of each specific bio-medical and psychosocial need may complicate discharge planning and transitions to other forms of follow-up care. In the absence of an extensive network of coordinated medical and behavioral health management, health systems are often unprepared for their needs. Follow-up for the addiction itself—with the introduction of well-grounded treatment programs, such as those that have evolved for medication-assisted treatment—may be lost. Care becomes reactive, focusing on the most acute and immediate need, rather than proactive.

For care to be proactive, it needs to focus on treating the whole disease of addiction—and that means treating the whole person behind the patient. In order for lifelong treatment to work, it needs to account for *life*—meaning the patient's physical health as well as what are generally referred to as social determinants of health (SDoH). While many in our industry do refer to these factors as social determinants of health, we take issue with the use of the term *determinants*. SDoH don't actually *determine* whether a patient recovers—they *influence* whether a patient recovers. Patients with difficult personal lives aren't doomed; we all have the capacity to get better. For this reason, we prefer to refer to these as *social aspects of health* (SAoH) rather than *social determinants of health*, but we will refer to these interchangeably throughout the book.

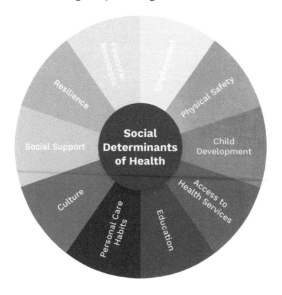

This graphic illustrates just how powerful SAoH can be in shaping a patient's health. The core aspects are far more heavily weighted toward one's social and financial supports as opposed to biological factors like genetics. In fact, clinical decisions made in response to lab or exam results account for only about 20 percent of the average person's healthcare. The other 80 percent of a person's health profile is determined by their lifestyle—which is why a strong behavioral health focus is crucial in SUD.

The Care Continuum from a Medical Perspective

Before addressing a holistic approach to SUD, we must address that the medical accompaniments to SUD are themselves complex. Any long-term approach to treatment is going to have to account for the fact that patients often require management of a variety of comorbidities and sequelae. Identifying and treating these additional conditions will help us manage the patient's SUD, while managing the patients' SUD will often help treat these comorbidities and prevent sequelae from occurring in the first place. As discussed earlier, there are many disease complications related to SUD.

As one example, people who suffer from opioid addiction and use heroin often develop hepatitis C, which leaves them predisposed to liver cancer, anemia, thyroid problems, and diabetes, among other illnesses.

So it might make sense to fold hepatitis C screening and treatment into SUD treatment, right? Unfortunately, this integration generally does not happen. Instead, Hepatitis C is usually managed as a separate disease state and very possibly by another specialist, known as a hepatologist.

Likewise, intravenous use of heroin directly correlates with the development of endocarditis, an infection of the lining of the heart. If prevention of endocarditis were considered at first contact with a person using heroin, the risk of this infection might be mitigated. Instead, like hepatitis C, this condition is usually managed separately—in this case, by cardiovascular specialists—and as it occurs. In fact, even tracking the rates of intravenous drug use–related endocarditis is complicated by the absence of a medical code for this diagnosis. To monitor rates of drug-related endocarditis in a hospital system, one needs to follow an algorithm to make that diagnostic association. How can we monitor success if it is difficult to identify in the first place?

These complications are not limited to opioid addiction. Alcohol use disorders, for example, can also lead to a multitude of conditions, including sclerosis of the liver, cirrhosis, liver cancer, cardiomyopathy, breast cancer, and pancreatitis. If someone has more than one substance use addiction and/or more than one disease sequela, they could be needing to see a multitude of specialists. Beyond this, in 70 percent of patients, SUD is also comorbid with mental health disorders. But these disorders are likewise often treated in isolation. Treatment for disease sequelae is rarely coordinated with treatment for the SUD.

Because of this oversight, we are missing tremendous opportunities for coordinated treatment that could prevent illnesses and improve the management of what conditions do develop. Instead of treating each disorder separately, we could be employing a holistic team approach to care delivery from the first window of opportunity, beginning at first contact with a patient (following an overdose, upon entering detox, etc.), as we do with diabetes treatment. Frequently, nutritionists, podiatrists, and experts in lifestyle management get involved to help a diabetic manage their chronic disease. That's not something that happens with SUD patients. We can and should be approaching follow-up care through an intensive, team-based strategy designed to support the patient and keep them in recovery. Recall the marathon analogy? We would be anticipating where patients require support and providing it along the way.

Instead, today, most follow-up fails to deliver this level of support. Instead, it typically involves a confusing, sometimes-overwhelming network of hospitals, medical providers, labs, social services, and more. The graphic demonstrates just how complicated any given patient's interaction within a single healthcare organization can get. This is to say nothing of the broader interactions with the community at large.

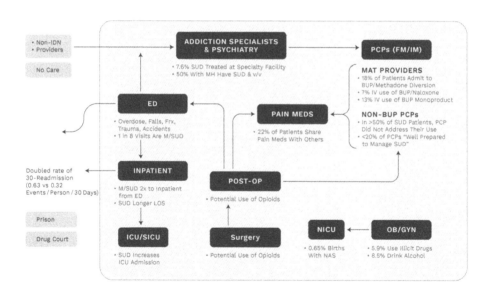

Navigating that is difficult enough, but if a patient is also struggling with comorbidities and/or sequelae—or is affected by negative SAoH, like food insecurity or poverty—the challenge to that patient grows exponentially. It's no wonder that as far back as 2001, the

Institute of Medicine called for "care coordination for patients across conditions, services and settings." Their research showed coordinated care—working together to provide patients with a system of support— boosts not only efficiency but also patient outcomes and satisfaction.

So why are these opportunities for improved care and better outcomes still being overlooked nearly twenty years later?

Part of the problem is a natural consequence of the siloing of these various aspects of care. This has led to limited integration across healthcare tools and technologies that would allow providers to understand what care opportunities can be leveraged. However, at the root of the problem remains stigma.

Despite the fact that addiction was classified by the American Medical Association as a disease back in 1987, the stigma associated with SUDs persists. On the patient side, it limits people's ability to fully embrace recovery, like they would if they had cancer or diabetes. Patients know there are things that they should do, yet they don't— often because they don't want to risk their reputations or because they aren't able to fully acknowledge their disease or their need for treatment to themselves.

Stigma also drove the regulatory problem we're dealing with today. We prioritized patient privacy so much that we developed strict regulatory pathways to protect SUD-related information through regulations such as 42 CFR Part 2. Although these regulations are evolving, they have been a severe impediment to the delivery of care, the coordination of care, and the ability to track and monitor success. Historically, these pathways have been so strict that they limit not only our ability to improve the field but also information that can impact direct patient care. If SUD had been truly perceived of as a chronic health condition, that type of regulation would not have been considered necessary.

However, once we start to reframe the way we think about this illness, we erode the root cause of our current, fragmented state of care—the stigma. That's when opportunities for better care emerge—care that allows for the sharing of critical health information; care that facilitates the necessary exchange of care needs and management across departments and institutions; and most importantly, care that addresses the whole patient, including the social aspects of health.

Social Aspects of Health

By taking a more holistic view of our patients' health, we can radically improve their treatment. However, as the chart below indicates, considerations beyond healthcare, like individual behavior and social and environmental factors, are more predictive when it comes to patient outcomes.

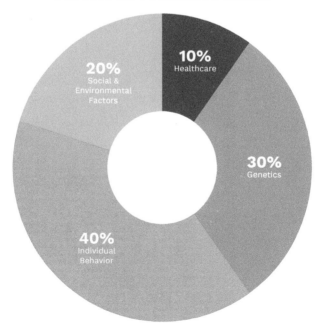

The Impact of Different Risk
Factors on Premature Death

10% Healthcare

20% Social & Environmental Factors

30% Genetics

40% Individual Behavior

To address the whole disease of addiction, we must take a more holistic view of our patients' lives. As we formulate a strategy for better SUD treatment, we have to acknowledge and address the powerful role that SAoH play in SUDs. Factors such as employment, residence, and relationships each have a profound influence on to what degree a patient struggles on their road to recovery.

How can we provide care that accounts for and addresses all the various factors affecting a single SUD patient in a coordinated, systemic fashion? How do we provide people suffering from addiction the level of support they need, just like HIV and cancer patients … and marathon runners?

The answer, as we see it, is employing a team approach within a coordinated system, similar to the one used by air traffic controllers.

Yes, air traffic controllers.

Chances are you immediately pictured a whole passel of harried people up in the tower at the airport, guiding planes as they take off and land. But the reality is that those people only make up a small fraction of the team responsible for the thousands of flights that take place in American air space every day. The vast majority of team members are working behind the scenes at big Federal Aviation Administration centers. Together with the controllers in the towers, they're able to coordinate what is arguably one of the most complicated logistical challenges in the world—delivering these planes and their passengers safely to their destinations. If you think about the scale of the operation, it's amazing it works almost flawlessly. But there's a reason for that—those people in the towers have a whole coordinated system that employs extensive technology and that massive team of people to help make sure they have the information to make the right call at the right moment.

That's where we have to do a better job—coordinating all the elements of SUD care into a single system where everything and everyone works together toward the same goal. To use a metaphor, the patient is like the pilot of a plane, whose destination is recovery. Meanwhile, the doctors, care coordinators, recovery coaches, sources of peer support, probation officers and treatment courts, licensed alcohol and drug counselors, addiction-treatment specialists, and MAT programs are like the workers on the tarmac, constantly double-checking the aircraft and making sure its airworthy and able to safely take the pilot where they want to go.

To make sure our system supports the patient in the best way possible and to avoid those missed opportunities we referenced earlier, we need to provide the care team with the tools and resources they need to measure every predictable and actionable aspect of a patient's recovery. Those include things like days without drug use, avoidance of triggers, ownership of use, and evidence of resiliency as well as the patient's personal SAoH to provide a view of the whole person behind the patient.

How Data Can Tell the Real Patient Story

The better we know a patient, the better we're able to understand their SAoH and what factors might affect their recovery. This is easiest when a patient engages and really opens up to treatment, allowing professionals the opportunity to interact more effectively and address SAoH more directly. Yes, recovery takes different paths; not every patient is at the point in their journey to recovery where they can freely acknowledge personal struggles. That's where data comes in. Data enables us to meet patients where they're at but still get the answers we need to provide an effective treatment plan. Collecting data also empowers us to treat both SUD and related behavioral health conditions from a standpoint of population health.

Data can come from a myriad of sources. Some data is common and regularly used, while other data sets are less obvious. For example, a common source of data may be a self-reported questionnaire about a patient's SAoH. The questionnaire becomes part of the record. Self-reported questionnaires may be augmented with less common but public sources of information that dig deeper into a patient's SAoH. There are accessible databases, including some that are privately funded, loaded with information that can tell us a lot about a patient's circumstances. Examples of public data include where a patient lives, whether they own a house, whether they've lost their license, and even how close they are to a grocery store. Obtain enough of this kind of information, and we get a fairly accurate picture of the patient's SAoH. Supplement these with analytical tools such as geo mapping or identifying hotspots, and there is a very powerful mechanism to support not only our patients but also the community as a whole.

This type of data is extremely valuable when treating SUD patients. It can be used to develop risk scores and take appropriate action on an individual patient—provided the patient is amenable. Yet even with a patient's hesitation, basic public information contained in these databases can provide the beginnings of a framework for a provider-patient discussion. For example, a provider might say, "Our records indicate you live at 25 Maple Street. Are you able to pick up food these days? I know that the grocery store on 6th Street closed recently...." This information can reveal food insecurities and transportation needs and allow a conversation between provider and patient.

Public data can tell providers information about a specific patient that allows care managers to stratify a single patient's risk; however, more importantly, aggregated data allows us to make assessments in assumption based on stratifying patients. Aggregate data reveals patterns in a specific patient demographic that may portend a risk of relapse and identifies certain kinds of behavior that may compromise the patient's road to recovery.

As much as people think they're unique, they're not. Individuals are often more alike than different, and specific patterns arise among us and our behaviors. While we recognize the individuality of each person, common categorizations can benefit our management of specific diseases and conditions. By considering trends, we can glean more insights that will inform better care. Proactive identification of these patterns can anticipate risks, highlight challenges individuals might face, and begin conversations for patients ready to tackle these observations.

Access to data facilitates population health management, which has a real chance of success. It allows us to make broad classifications, group patients based on similar attributes, ask the right questions, and put risk-stratified patients on certain types of treatment plans.

Incorporation of SAoH-related data even enables holistic management of the disease itself, meaning the continuum of care, care coordination, and environmental and genetic factors may play a role in disease progression and treatment. Recent guidance from the Centers for Medicare and Medicaid Services (CMS) has been issued to advocate for the management of SAoH. There are six commonly recognized domains that require specific attention.

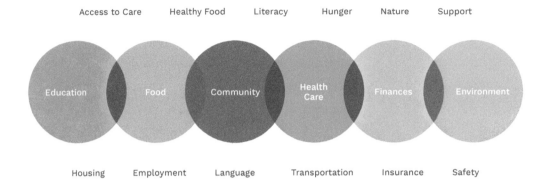

Access to Care   Healthy Food   Literacy   Hunger   Nature   Support

Education   Food   Community   Health Care   Finances   Environment

Housing   Employment   Language   Transportation   Insurance   Safety

USING TECHNOLOGY-ASSISTED CARE

For a provider to be able to use all this information, they have to get it, digest it, and know how to use it. How are they supposed to do that?

Providers don't have time to scour databases and analyze long lists of information. To put this treasure trove of data to use, they need tools and technology that highlights information in a user-friendly, digestible, and actionable way. These tools have traditionally been very siloed, just like care teams are siloed, which makes it difficult for any single provider to see the whole patient.

But software platforms and workflow tools that share information across an entire care team can give each provider a more holistic view of the patient. As one example, our organization has developed one such technology-assisted care (TAC) solution, called Navigator. Navigator provides insight into a patient's day-to-day life by sitting on top of already existing electronic health records. It uses data to spotlight red-flag areas and identify activities that promote well-being.

Facilitation of the daily management of SUD is arguably far more pressing than as seen with other chronic diseases. First, its intersection with physical health is complex, demonstrating frequent comorbidities and extensive disease sequelae. Second, the overlay of SAoH further complicates the clinical picture. Finally, the impact of the disease on decision-making, judgment, and disclosure can add yet another layer.

Any electronic management system must begin with a simple patient profile. Through incorporation of patient questionnaires, publicly available datasets, and other forms of data, one can aggregate information on a particular population and monitor the activities of that population. For providers to transcend crisis management and enter into the world of long-term treatment, providers have to begin learning more about the lives of their patients, incorporating more patient data into care workflows and decision-making processes. The data generated by technology-assisted care solutions can give them an overview of their patients' lives, so they can see where they fit into the world and what obstacles they're likely to face.

Some providers already ask patients about those obstacles. For example, one might try to discover what is keeping an individual from getting to treatment or counseling. They may even provide the patient with a gas card or bus pass to support them if transportation is an issue. However, even these providers are not likely to be capturing the intervention in a systematic enough way as to measure its impact.

> A comprehensive solution requires providers have access to holistic data at their fingertips.

It's not just about what limits a patient's access to care but what will drive success in their overall recovery. A comprehensive solution requires providers have access to holistic data at their fingertips. Most providers don't have the time or bandwidth to derive all that data on their own; instead, technology-assisted care solutions can be used to gather data in advance. With this information in hand, caregivers can formulate specific questions about known predictors of treatment success to develop a program tailored to the patient's personal needs.

FREE WILL

To explain the devastating changes in behavior of a person who is addicted, such that even the most severe threat of punishment is insufficient to keep them from taking drugs—where they are willing to give up *everything they care for* in order to take a drug—it is not enough to say that addiction is a chronic brain disease. What we mean by that is something very specific and profound: that because of drug use, a person's brain is no longer able to produce something needed for our functioning and that healthy people take for granted, *free will.*

—Nora Volkow, Director, National Institute on Drug Abuse

To be truly a useful technology solution, however, critical components are necessary. In addition to data access, solutions must include interventions, such as lists of community resources that can be leveraged. Further, incorporation of clinical protocols into the technology allows for optimized clinical workflows, managing provider time efficiently and revealing the most critical clinical steps.

While there are many new technology solutions that are evolving each day, we remain beholden to the availability of integrated data streams and to policymakers who must reform antiquated regulatory limitations on data sharing in the field of mental health that are based in fear and stigma. These advancements are necessary to truly realize the benefits of this technology.

Beyond coordinating care, a technology solution would be further impactful if it could dramatically improve the level of patient engagement when that care is received.

The Benefits of Patient Engagement

When we learn more about the lives of our patients, we are much better positioned to engage those patients in their own care. That in turn boosts our chances of keeping those patients on the recovery track.

Historically, SUD patients have been beaten down by the stigma around addiction. In addition, the disease itself wreaks havoc on their lives and the lives of those around them. With the chemical rewiring of their brain, patients have lost the ability to control their decision-making when it comes to the use of their drug of choice. Because our society hasn't quite determined how to effectively support these patients, we add to that beat down by restricting choices for patients as they go further along in their disease state.

It's akin to how parents manage their kids. If they're doing okay, we give them all the freedom in the world. But if they're starting to struggle with some aspect of their lives (say, their grades or maybe hanging out with a dangerous crowd), we start to narrow their choices. We restrict freedoms to encourage them to be more responsible. This is the same way we've attempted as a society to manage the addiction problem. But at the end of the day, it leaves the patient population in a position of not having a lot of choice in how they manage their condition.

For example, if a person is arrested for carrying a small amount of a drug like cocaine, they are placed before a judge and given a choice between going to jail and going into treatment. Obviously, they're going to pick treatment because they don't want to go to jail. But they're not really picking treatment. They're forced into treatment without much choice or empowerment—a scenario that doesn't exactly set the stage for engagement.

With this background, finding a way to boost engagement and empowerment in care delivery is not only important but also, at times, received as a relatively novel (and welcome) feeling for patients. The importance of patient engagement is not lost on treatment providers. Many techniques, like motivational interviewing and similar strategies, have been deployed for years. However, the criticality of this component to treatment may not be as deeply understood by all providers and community organizations supporting SUD patients. Further, the extent to which we can engage patients—not only in discussions about their use but in the myriad decisions and ways in which we impact them—is generally not fully appreciated.

In our own work in the laboratory setting, we came across an unconventional example related to empowerment. Prior to the Obama administration, when we performed urine collection for drug tests, it was sex matched. If a patient came in as a woman, they were paired with a woman and the observed collection was done according to certain protocols. Then federal mandates stated a patient's own gender identity should trump their biological sex in healthcare, so the process was gender matched. That meant asking the patient, "Do you identify as male or female?" They instead received the protocol based on how they self-identified.

LINKAGE CLINICAL TRIAL

The LINKAGE intervention taught skills to help patients communicate effectively with physicians and engage in their healthcare using the EHR as a platform.

—Weisner et al., *JAMA Psychiatry*, 2016

That one simple question was very empowering for some patients. They had a choice about how they were going to get their urine collection done. Though it was a small piece of their care, it gave them agency and allowed them to make a choice. In a world where they're often not allowed to make many choices, this was impactful.

In fact, this patient population would benefit greatly from empowerment. There are many choices they can make that don't undermine treatment but still allow them to start seeing themselves as capable of making good decisions. Their self-esteem and self-efficacy grow correspondingly.

OTHER WAYS TO ENGAGE

Engaging patients in their care can be as simple as making them a part of it.

A recent study in *JAMA Psychiatry* investigated the effects of patient engagement and intervention strategies in alcohol and other addictions. This work, out of Kaiser Permanente of Northern California, demonstrated that digital, interactive patient-engagement programs were superior to the standard of care. Patients were divided into two groups at a large outpatient facility. One group received regular care, and one group received intervention care through

LINKAGE, a system that uses electronic health records and patient portals to engage patients. The team found that the group participating in LINKAGE had higher levels of patient satisfaction and improved relationships with their providers.

According to the research team, "LINKAGE participants had more days of patient portal log-in, including seeking medical advice, receiving messages from primary care physicians, checking on laboratory test results, and reviewing medical information."[16]

Opportunities for a patient to increase engagement with their treatment can be as close as their smartphone. Smartphones are an ideal platform for delivering messaging and education since most people rely on them so heavily. Patients can receive messages that empower them to manage their meetings and appointments or share tips and advice to motivate them to stay on track.

Education is even more powerful than messaging. One of the best ways to educate is through games, especially when it comes to reaching young adults. And smartphones are also an ideal platform for games.

For instance, if a patient is going to be prescribed an opioid painkiller, a mobile game can train them to take their medication correctly and avoid developing an addiction. Education is an effective preventative tool cautioning against pitfalls of opioid use, identifying warning signs of addiction, and reengaging with help if things begin to feel unmanageable. Given the ubiquity of smartphone apps, this type of platform could easily be applied to helping someone manage their recovery.

The way we see it, increased patient engagement will also happen naturally as a byproduct of better care coordination. It's not

---

16   Chi, Weisner, et al. "Examination of the Effects of an Intervention Aiming to Link Patients Receiving Addiction Treatment with Health Care: The LINKAGE Clinical Trial," *JAMA Psychiatry* 73, no. 8 (2016): 804–814, https://jamanetwork.com/journals/jamapsychiatry/fullarticle/2527960.

just about gadgets and bells and whistles. It's about people—people who understand the patient, who care enough about them to see the patient as a whole person, and who are all working together to deliver the very best care to help that patient get through recovery. Just like marathon runners, it's the least they deserve.

For us to effectively deliver lifelong care, we need to develop an approach to care that takes into account our patients' actual lives. We need treatment to be based on their complete health profiles as well as their day-to-day lifestyles. It's time to look beyond lab results and dig deeper into who these patients are and what they're all about. Only this kind of disruptive, innovative effort will make a significant difference. As we further adopt different financial models for the delivery of healthcare, such as value-based care, this holistic view becomes increasingly important.

Cam Lauf, whose story we shared earlier, has joined in this effort in his position as Executive Director at the Turning Point Center of Chittenden County in Vermont and emergency department recovery coaching program supervisor at the University of Vermont. He discusses how patient engagement can make a big difference.

> When somebody comes into the ED, we work with them and help them access treatment. We educate them about the realistic experience of what treatment looks like, depending on whatever substance they're struggling with. We discuss modalities, we discuss acuity of what use is, and we really just give them a breakdown on their substance use and the education around that. And then what we do is we say, "Hey, you know, I feel as if you really got a lot out of our conversation, I really appreciate you, and I really value you for opening up to us. You're going through a lot right

now. Would you want for us to call you regularly?" And what that does is open the door for that person to have a continuous engagement with a positive reinforcing factor toward change.

It's full empowerment. It's a patient-centered focus that gives them full autonomy. That creates a catalyst for their self-actualization post-discharge from the ED and their own autonomy moving forward.

Our message is, "Hey, we don't really care what you do. We care about you, and we see value in you, and we believe that you can see value in yourself, but what you do moving forward, that's on you. We're here just to support you in whatever decision that you make and help you feel like you're not alone in this. Having that continued engagement of somebody who understands recovery and who knows the system, who you can bounce ideas off of, or somebody who bugs the shit out of you … no matter what the relationship is, you can always come back to them. We focus on the positives of the situation and lessen the stigma.

While we want to fully empower patients, they should not feel that they need to carry these burdens alone. In the words of Lisa Olivera, "Just because no one can heal or do your inner work for you, doesn't mean you can, should or need to do it alone." There are many resources currently available to patients; the key is to leverage them—the care providers, community events and other resources and technology.

In the next chapter, we'll learn more about how treating the whole person can influence treatment results and we'll reveal the power data can have to elevate and facilitate a holistic care approach.

CHAPTER FOUR

THERE'S POWER IN NUMBERS

You can have data without information, but you cannot have information without data.

—DANIEL KEYS MORAN

At present, our approach to SUD care is largely transactional.

Care focuses on delivering direct, individualized patient care on a day-to-day basis. In SUD, transactional care dominates and limits the ability of providers to rise above what they're doing and see the bigger picture.

SUD care is often provided through a string of transactions, including multidisciplinary transactions, with little to no coordination between providers and community resources. Each session, appointment, and visit is a one-off interaction. The overburdened care team may find it difficult to see beyond this single consultation. This compromises the lasting value of the interaction, limiting future strategies for better care delivery.

For example, let's consider a patient who missed an appointment for MAT therapy on Monday. At Tuesday's multidisciplinary team meeting, all care providers discuss the fact that that patient's lack of transportation kept them from coming to the doctor. Because they're deeply committed to this patient's care, the entire team spends ten minutes talking about that one patient and that one problem. Considering the other time constraints, this is a heavy lift for the team. It's valuable work: it's just not necessarily the most efficient path forward ... or the best use of their time.

These transactional strategies are promoted by how our health system is reimbursed. Unfortunately, as the opioid epidemic accelerates in the face of the COVID-19 pandemic, we don't have the luxury to wait for the gradual shift from fee-for-service to a value-based care model. We need to consider other tactical solutions in the interim. Let's consider the prior example of the tactical work in the MAT program: What if there were an automated mechanism to channel that patient into a resource for their transportation? What if there were a solution that could have been launched on Monday instead of Tuesday, not discussed for ten minutes by five to seven people, and already responded to the patient to give them the help they needed? The transportation problem would have been solved in real time, and the care team could have spent its time on other issues.

Our transactional system of care means providers often aren't maximizing SAoH in their care or looking at the patient holistically. While most providers are aware of the importance of SAoH, these are highly underused. Culturally, we may even overestimate how much we capitalize on SAoH. Most care teams ask about transportation and access to care. However, this is not using SAoH to see the bigger picture in order to improve patient care; care access discussions are focused on how to get the patient back for their next visit. This focus is centered on clinical operations and setting up the next transaction rather than focusing on the patient's long-term needs.

We recognize that these are important issues. Dedicating time and energy to one patient's transportation is very personal, and it shows a level of commitment to that patient. But it promotes more transactions rather than a holistic approach to care. Further, it's a one-off solution. Once the team solves that one patient's one problem, so many remain.

Unfortunately, most providers are locked into this model of transactional care because they don't have a choice. The system is overwhelmed. They don't have the tools, the technology, and the support to look at the bigger picture of their patients' lives. As a result, we aren't giving patients as much value as we could be. We aren't elevating our care with technology that enables us to have a consolidation point for data analytics. Our failure to do so has cost us dearly—socially and financially.

How Data Elevates Care

To understand how data improves care, let's consider other diseases that have leveraged data. For decades, diabetes and cancer care has been informed by an abundance of data. Masses of research have been collected on large populations, creating a tremendous amount of data. This data informs the development of benchmarks and protocols that drive care. As we provide care, we collect more data. It's a circle that constantly feeds itself, so the care continually evolves and improves. For patients with cancer and diabetes, the data will continue to inform protocols, inspire adjustments, and lead to better care for other patients.

With behavioral health and SUD, we haven't had the luxury of being part of that circle of expanding knowledge. Due, in part, to stigma and the way care has evolved, much of addiction care and opioid care is done on the fringes of the core healthcare system. Historically, when you work on the fringes, the pay, the resources, and the visibility that flow your way suffer.

Second, without resources, there isn't investment in the tools and infrastructure that can provide a long-term view that helps inform care. For example, a great deal of money has been committed to cancer over the years. Historically, behavioral health and SUD have received less. Providers haven't been able to invest in strategies that allow them to build a population health system for behavioral health conditions in the same way we have for cancer patients.

A third consideration is that many of those that provide care to patients with SUD are not formally trained in addiction medicine but are intersecting with acute care needs of the patients. The provision of crisis care or time-delimited medical services doesn't allow for long-term patient management. If you have a chronic condition like diabetes or cancer, you may enter the system knowing you're going to get long-term care. Your condition will be managed for as long as you have the condition, which often means for the rest of your life, with a goal of maintaining optimal quality of life for as long as possible.

Finally, regulatory limits on sharing data—fueled by well-intentioned privacy laws that, sadly, are promoted by a fear of stigma—also limit the ability to collect data and drive analytics. Too much of this information is locked away, sequestering meaningful SUD-related health information; limiting access; and precluding evidence-based research to strengthen the delivery of care.

Miro Weinberger, mayor of Burlington, Vermont, articulates some of these limitations:

One of my great frustrations is we don't really know in an empirical way what causes people to drop out of treatment. At least I don't … The first thing we're doing is really trying to answer that question with the data. The data is just a mess, in part, because of the medical privacy concerns, as well as the fact that every organization keeps its own data. It's definitely not coordinated. So that's what we're working on now. We're trying to get everybody to be measuring retention in the same way, so that we're speaking a congruent language. And we're trying to get people to be much better about recording why people leave, what the outcomes are, and do that in consistent ways.

The lack of a longitudinal approach, a robust infrastructure, and well-supported resources has limited our ability to draw on standard tools used for other parts of medical care. Care delivery has been wonderfully individualized and tailored but lacks the core definitions of success, agreed-upon outcome targets, and a rugged set of approaches that are universally deployed.

> The lack of a longitudinal approach, a robust infrastructure, and well-supported resources has limited our ability to draw on standard tools used for other parts of medical care.

Pete Mumma is the president and CEO of Phoenix House New England, a provider of inpatient and outpatient care across nine US states. He sees the value of collecting data so we can measure outcomes and focus on what works. He talks about the evolution of its mission.

Phoenix House was founded in the late fifties, early sixties as a therapeutic community for people. That's where the tools existed at the time. It was basically sober houses for people who want to straighten themselves up and it was more about tough love. But over time, science grew and we understood there were evidence-based pathways to treat folks. So treatment became healthcare rather than therapeutic communities. We still do use therapeutic community techniques and groups and milieu treatment and things like that, but it's really much more evidence based.

[One thing] we could really benefit from in this industry is: what does it mean to be excellent? We see the private for-profit sites claiming all the time they're the best in the world … but when you look at it, outcomes are very difficult to show with the kind of data that a private for-profit or a small not-for-profit doesn't have access to.

Many of the answers lie in the large data and how we're measuring our outcomes. They should be measured through very empirical measures and should answer the question, are people improving their lives? And how are we leveraging test results across the whole gestalt of the person, rather than just that a patient has a positive urine screen?... We want to correlate that with what else was going on in the client's life at that time. Are they diabetic? Did they have an episode? If they had a cardiac issue, did they have an episode with that?

That's where data becomes information that can become knowledge. Until we can move further down that pipeline, we're just chasing numbers. Who's to say whether what's correlative, causal or just happenstance until we can really start to put those big numbers together?

Numbers are Real People and Impacted Lives

Besides lacking data, there has been a divide between behavioral health and primary care, with differential biases within those systems on how to manage disease states. At times, differences are structural, with behavioral health handled by clinicians, counselors, and social workers and medical conditions addressed by nurse practitioners and physicians. Each discipline uses a different set of tool kits, along with different sets of systemic biases that evolve out of those differences.

As authors, we witnessed these biases firsthand in 2015, when we attended one of the most prominent addiction-centered conferences in the country. As we went from lecture to lecture, we were struck by the absence of any data in the presentations. This is simply unheard of for a medical conference—at a conference on any other topic, the lectures are all about data. But at this conference, they were all about experiences and anecdotes.

When we finally found ourselves at a lecture that presented data, we were excited. When it was over, we turned to another attendee and said, "Oh, that was really interesting; that was different because it was real. There was a lot of data." But the guy sitting next to us had a totally different impression of what they had both experienced. He said, "Yeah, they missed the mark because this is really about personalized tailored care."

This exchange highlights a significant barrier to applying the benefits of a population health approach to patient care: the resistance to "reducing the SUD patient to a number." There's something about the brain and behaviors that makes people hesitate to be categorical and systematic when it comes to SUD and behavioral healthcare. Behavioral health issues are so personal, and there's such a history of stigma attached to them that, historically, we have not approached addiction care like that of other medical conditions. While we recognize everyone's unique individuality and the amalgam of their experiences, we are depriving patients of the most effective care possible without a greater reliance on data.

Population health isn't about diminishing the ability to personalize care. It's using data to identify and tailor treatments to strategic populations, to stratify patients with regard to what their next outcomes are going to be, and to develop a more insightful approach to care. It is an approach that predicts outcomes and preempts obstacles. It enables providers to focus more on each patient's individual needs and provide them with better care.

With data, we can implement real population-health-level approaches, monitor outcomes, and replicate those plans across the country for consistency, health, outcomes, and programs—and ultimately channel money into programs that work.

Case Study: Improving Breast Cancer Patient Outreach in California

Data can assist those who desperately need it. There are a multitude of success stories along these lines, but let's put the spotlight on one for the moment.

Tracking California, a program of the nonprofit Public Health Institute, recognized that a lack of data on breast cancer cases in the state was making it difficult to identify those most in need of medical treatment. The data that was being shared was analyzed for the state as a whole or at the county level. But this information was not granular enough. Without specific city- and neighborhood-level data, it was difficult to target the areas where the need was greatest.

With that in mind, Tracking California put together an advisory board of breast cancer advocates, clinicians, and public health agencies to determine the best way to map breast cancer data for the state. When mapping areas at the town and town section levels, they found some surprises. For example, portions of East Ventura and West Los Angeles showed a larger-than-normal number of breast cancer cases. County-level rates didn't demonstrate any problems in these areas. In these two geographically restricted neighborhoods, women who were diagnosed with invasive breast cancer were more likely to lack health insurance or receive governmental assistance.

An oncology nurse at a hospital in East Ventura, one of the areas with a high rate of incidents, was intrigued with the new data-driven approach and invited Tracking California to present the findings to their breast cancer leadership committee. After the presentation, the committee used the results to focus outreach and education on low-income clients who needed help, incorporating breast cancer–specific messaging into their efforts and enabling them to shine a light on the hidden needs of women in their community.[17]

Along similar lines, Health Quality Partners has worked with a coalition of doctors, nurses, social workers, outreach specialists, and data analysts since 2001 to research and deploy advanced preventative care models for the elderly. By reallocating resources to high-needs, high-cost patients, it has managed to reduce mortality among the older population of southeastern Pennsylvania by 25 percent.[18]

---

17   "California's Success Improving Breast Cancer Patient Outreach and Education," CDC, accessed September 1, 2021, https://www.cdc.gov/nceh/tracking/success/california.htm.

18   "Success Stories," Health Catalyst, accessed September 1, 2021, https://www.healthcatalyst.com/population-health-documentary-showcases-success-stories.

How Data Informs Individualized Care

A real-time example of the use of population health data in informing patient care can be found with the COVID-19 pandemic. Contact tracing and testing surveillance help inform us if a sore throat is COVID or postnasal drip from allergies. Even with all the well-documented failures of our government to deal with the COVID-19 crisis, our response has showcased the power of data analytics.

Let's make a big admission here—when we physicians make diagnoses, we may not be certain of their accuracy. We weigh the facts, make our best diagnostic assessment, and treat according to that diagnosis. Unfortunately, providers are human and, all too often, can display an unconscious bias that interferes with the correct diagnosis. For example, in medical school, we used to joke that any of our own symptoms could mean we had the disease we'd just learned about. This is known as "availability heuristic"—we are swayed by what we already know and what we can readily draw up to make a diagnostic call. Younger or less practiced physicians may be more subject to it, but it is certainly true that we all rely upon it. As shown in the figure, there is a lot we get out of it.

Heuristics

- Limit Mental Effort
- May Support Problem Solving
- Simplify
- Can Be Fast & Accurate

Unfortunately, we can also misjudge a patient's health issues. That's why the more information we have, the better our diagnosis and the more suitable our treatment strategy will be. Numbers don't lie. While it's true that data can be manipulated, it provides a fact-based overview that can't be dismissed if the data is rigorously vetted.

That's why tracking patients' health data, like we're doing with COVID-19, allows us to remove some of the uncertainty from our treatment choices: We can glean powerful insights into what works and what doesn't, creating bedside analytic tools that will inform treatment strategies. We can also deepen our understanding of our patients' needs and empower the treatment of SAoH through the following ways:

Value Proposition for Population Health-Level Data

Reveal Data	Find Patterns	Set Protocols	Preempt Interventions	Track Outcomes	Predict Behaviors	Manage Risk

➡ Revealing data that's not readily accessible in a short clinical visit

Some information may not be apparent to either the patient or the provider. For example, it may not occur to the patient that their diet might suffer simply by not living close to a grocery store that sells fresh fruits and vegetables. Instead, they might rely on a local minimart at a gas station, where the healthy choices are obviously few and far between.

➡ Empowering ourselves to find patterns

Population health data allows us to categorically bin signs, symptoms, and behaviors that we can apply to other patients. This helps us determine how to diagnose those patients and deliver the appropriate care.

➡ Setting protocols

Let's say a patient is going into orthopedic surgery, where they will be prescribed opioids. The provider could execute a treatment plan that tracks and manages that opioid use. If a patient is in crisis, a provider might call for future checkups, urine tests, group therapy, and a wellness seminar. In both cases, we can track these protocols for their effectiveness.

➡ Preempting interventions

A patient in crisis may have recently lost their driver's license. The lack of transportation could become an obstacle to recovery because it becomes much more difficult to get to group therapy or a wellness seminar. If the provider has data that includes the fact the patient lacks a license, that knowledge can be used to coach the patient through the challenge they're facing, perhaps by recommending alternative modes of transportation or reassigning them to a more accessible therapy location.

➡ Tracking outcomes

We can track the correlation between specific treatment options and recovery outcomes, investigating, for example, how patients fare when they attend one type of group therapy versus another. This data can then be used to negotiate with payers by providing concrete evidence that a particular strategy delivers a higher value and is worth a deeper investment.

→ Predicting behaviors

We know some people on opioid prescriptions don't develop addictions when others do, that some people with opioid addictions escalate to heroin use when others don't, and that some heroin users develop hepatitis C when others develop no sequelae at all. We can, on our own, try to make intuitive assumptions about what sets each group apart, but they are still *assumptions* if data is not available. By contrast, with that data in hand, we can stratify patients, predict outcomes, prevent addiction, and preempt crises.

EPIDEMIC WITHIN A PANDEMIC

Mental distress during the pandemic is occurring against a backdrop of high rates of mental illness and substance use that existed prior to the current crisis.... The pandemic has both short- and long-term implications for mental health and substance use, particularly for groups at risk of new or exacerbated mental health disorders and those facing barriers to accessing care.

—Panchal et al., KFF, February 2021

→ Managing risk

The use of data allows us to anticipate challenges our patients may face and mitigate their impact. The more we know, the more we can do to alleviate obstacles to recovery and prevent episodic crisis points.

As we said earlier, a doctor's diagnosis is not foolproof—it can be a best guess. A behavioral health diagnosis is especially challenging: there are fewer objective measures for diagnosis and treatment success than many of the physical health counterparts. Beyond that lack of objective measurements, it may be difficult to get the full story from the patient. Due to stigma and fear, patients may be reluctant to disclose the extent of their condition. The issue itself may prevent the patient from clearly articulating what they're feeling. And there is the not-insignificant matter of federal regulations that require confidentiality when it comes to the records of those with SUD.

Finally, we must address the healthcare industry's favored approach when it comes to behavioral-health diagnoses: the heavy emphasis on individualized care. While this approach enables us to put laser focus on a given patient, it risks omission of important variables, such as SAoH and the comorbidities that influence that individualized care. It also doesn't allow for any evaluation of effectiveness of any given treatment intervention. We are unable to leverage insights from patterns across populations. A population approach can leverage prior experiences to the benefit of the patient before us. Once we have this population-level view, its use in combination with personalized care will enable us to tackle any crisis.

> Once we have this population-level view, its use in combination with personalized care will enable us to tackle any crisis.

The Urgent Need for More Behavioral-Health-Related Data

At the moment, we're dealing with a dramatic rise in behavioral health and SUD issues during the COVID-19 pandemic. We should expect this to get worse.

More than ever, we must have the tools in place to deal with the collateral impact of substantial societal events. For example, during the economic downturn that began in late 2008, the suicide rate in the US and Europe rose substantially.[19] We can predict a similar outcome will result from the pandemic and the economic impact that has followed. We must use data and analytics in a new way to help manage the population and the patients more effectively.

For some time, institutions have been building protocols to manage cardiovascular disease, thrombosis, myocardial infarction, and other physical ailments. The behavioral health field, however, is behind other disciplines, and care for SUD will benefit greatly from a data-driven, protocol-based approach.

Driving protocol development can be difficult at first—we are asking providers to come together and agree on how to manage patient populations. This may be a tricky proposition. Often, we providers draw upon all the exceptions to the rule—because for our patient, the 80-20 rule (80 percent of effects come from 20 percent of the causes) isn't good enough. As consensus is driven, however, we've found that the 80-20 rule is not a bad place to start. It helps you map out the workflow and what the patient needs, allowing for modifications from there.

The protocol needs to be a living process, and this is often where the rubber meets the road. It can't be a document sitting on the provider's desktop or some other document repository. It needs to be *used*. Strong leadership can promote adoption of each step along the way. Alternatively, technology-assisted care can promote adoption by deploying checklists, preestablished workflows, and unified workstreams.

---

19   Maanvi Singh, "Suicide Rate in US and Europe Climbed During Great Recession," NPR, June 11, 2014, https://www.npr.org/sections/krulwich/2014/06/11/318885533/suicide-rate-in-u-s-and-europe-climbed-during-great-recession.

This standardized approach is a way to start. From there, we find there are multiple pathways to choose from, based on a patient's risk, other health conditions, and socioeconomic and living influencers that drive care delivery. This allows for multiple approaches that have drawn upon the original approach and solving the 80 percent. There is still your unique patient—the 20 percent. You have a way to approach the patient based on evidence and known factors; you know what can influence treatment success and then tailor it to your patient's case.

Big Data will never evolve into the be-all and end-all when it comes to SUD patients. We providers are not computers because, frankly, computers can't do as good a job as we can when it comes to diagnosing and caring for patients. There are a lot of reasons for this, but mostly it boils down to the human connection that allows us to delve deeper into behavioral health issues. However, there is a lot that Big Data can do to *inform* our care and help us affirm our assessments.

Care Impact of Data

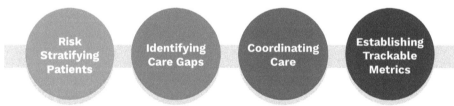

Pete Mumma of Phoenix House New England offers perspective on what he envisions:

> I want to build a better way for treatment to occur. I want to build better networks so that we can all hopefully get ahead of this thing and bring a new systematic approach. I think semantics are important—SUDs aren't cured, but

with a different set of resources, we can address problems in a new way and hopefully get people to help patients get themselves to a place where they are experiencing new and better outcomes in their lives.

I think it's going to take a fair system and entities being willing to embrace that these problems exist in our communities and in our systems, whether we want to address them or not. Not addressing them is still a choice. It may not be the choice that major systems, hospital systems or state government systems or other systems want to embrace. But by saying, we're going to underfund these things, or we're going to focus on cancer care or OB-GYN or whatever the issue is, the overdose epidemic is going to continue.

I dream of a day when the system doesn't encourage patients to get boxed into a path, but rather helps them address their own issues on an individualized basis, creating a solution path for each individual that's unique and tailored for them—because it's the only thing that's going to work.

SUD is an incredibly complex disorder. Whether a person develops the condition, recovers, or relapses, this individual is dependent on a host of external factors. Development of long-term treatment strategies, improvement in outcomes, and focus on external factors are all paramount to our collective success. Big Data is critical to shifting the current paradigm.

Tracking patient treatments and outcomes will also help to calculate the total cost of care, which, as we'll see in the next chapter, is an essential step toward improving care.

CHAPTER FIVE

SETTING A STICKER PRICE

Healing is an art, medicine is a science, and healthcare is a business.

—AMR ABOULISH, MD

In the last chapter, we looked at why data is so important to formulating new and effective protocols for behavioral health and SUD treatment. In this chapter, we're going to look at another crucial element—money.

This chapter should provide a backdrop for both the financial pressures and the operational inefficiencies that face medical care generally today. While much of this chapter addresses healthcare financial stewardship in general, many of these issues are most pressing in the behavioral health space, which has historically been underfunded and not fully integrated into routine medical practice.

There is a vast gulf between the theoretical and the practical: you can brainstorm the greatest innovations in history, but when it comes to bringing them to life, you end up battling a whole host of opponents. As articulated by Innovate Vancouver, there are a host of foes.

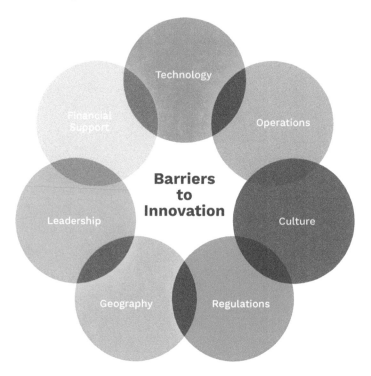

Perhaps the most formidable of those opponents is a lack of financing to implement innovations in a meaningful manner.

Our health system can be both inefficient and costly, making meaningful change difficult to achieve. As described in the quote that opens this chapter—healthcare is a *business* much like any other. Even when we're talking about nonprofit organizations, organizations may be motivated by the bottom line like many other industries, such as banking, real estate, and car manufacturing. As a business, we aren't doing so well.

Source: Lucian Leape, M.D. Image: Advisory Board Company. (2005). In Schwartz's Principles of Surgery (9 ed.). Doi: 10.1007/s00268-010-0447-y. [Digitale image]. Retrieved May 15, 2018.

At first, this can be discouraging. After all, robust healthcare is necessary to ensure our collective well-being. Yet as financial pressures mount in healthcare, the bottom line may be increasingly critical and decisive.

If we want to craft an effective holistic and sustainable approach to tackling behavioral health, we *must* calculate costs as accurately and realistically as possible. Otherwise, we're risking a ride to Fantasyland. We are simply not going to be able to create practical treatment strategies until we can accurately measure their cost, including both financial and health-related costs.

This chapter will provide an overview of the current healthcare

> Collectively, we are aiming for a higher quality of care, better results, and lower costs for our behavioral health patients.

financial picture and a method of breaking down those costs so that we can craft efficient and coordinated treatment paths that will provide more bang for the buck. Collectively, we are aiming for a higher quality of care, better results, and lower costs for our behavioral health patients.

The Mounting Cost of Healthcare

To recognize just how much money matters in healthcare, consider the list of the top ten profitable industries in America in 2020.[20]

Top 10 Profitable Industries in America in 2020

Rank	Business	Total 2020 Profit
1	Commercial Banking	$165.6 B
2	Trusts and Estates	$127.0 B
3	Commercial Leasing	$104.0 B
4	Hospitals	$92.7 B
5	Portfolio Management	$89.0 B
6	Health & Medical Insurance	$84.5 B
7	Private Equity & Investment Vehicles	$75.5 B
8	Real Estate Investment Trusts	$73.1 B
9	Law Firms	$68.4 B
10	Real Estate Loans & Collateralized Debt in US	$60.8 B

Source: IBISWorld

Shocked to find both hospitals and health insurance in the top ten? This underscores that the field of medicine is very much a business in America, and like any other business, it must be sustainable. Financial stewardship is an integral part of the delivery of care.

---

20   "Most Profitable Industries in the US in 2021," IBISWorld, accessed September 1, 2021, https://www.ibisworld.com/united-states/industry-trends/most-profitable-industries/.

The cost of care has been ballooning for decades. For example, in 1960, healthcare accounted for only 5 percent of the GDP; but by 2018, that percentage had skyrocketed to 18 percent.[21] In 2018, we spent $3.6 trillion on healthcare, far exceeding almost every other country in the world.

"In spite of all the efforts in the US to control health spending over the past 25 years, the story remains the same—the US remains the most expensive because of the prices the US pays for health services," says Bloomberg School professor Gerard Anderson.[22]

The high cost of US healthcare affects both the sick and the well. Increasing healthcare expenditures have depressed consumers' spending power for the past few decades. Even though salaries for most American workers have risen, their net pay has stayed stagnant because the price of health insurance keeps rising.[23]

AVERAGE SPENDING

America spends about 8 percent of healthcare dollars on administrative costs, compared to 1-3 percent in other developed countries.

21 "Why Are Americans Paying More for Healthcare?" Peter G. Peterson Foundation, April 20, 2020, https://www.pgpf.org/blog/2020/04/why-are-americans-paying-more-for-healthcare.

22 "Americans on Average Continue to Spend Much More for Health Care—While Getting Less Care—than People in Other Developed Countries," Johns Hopkins, accessed September 1, 2021, https://publichealth.jhu.edu/2019/us-health-care-spending-highest-among-developed-countries.

23 Alex Kacik, "Hospital Price Growth Driving Healthcare Spending," Modern Healthcare, February 4, 2019, https://www.modernhealthcare.com/article/20190204/NEWS/190209984/hospital-price-growth-driving-healthcare-spending.

The online publication Investopedia identified six reasons why US healthcare is so much more expensive than that of other countries:[24]

1. Out-of-control administrative costs

While we don't fully subscribe to the words of Walter Cronkite, "America's healthcare system is neither healthy, caring, nor a system," we recognize that administrative costs are astounding due the complexity of its processes. These administrative costs are frequently cited as a cause for excess medical spending.

The US system is complex, with distinct rules, funding, enrollment dates, out-of-pocket costs for private and employer-based insurance, and tiers of coverage to choose from. Plans may or may not include prescription drug coverage, which has its own complexities. It's not just the average person whose head starts spinning from these different systems; providers also drown in paperwork dealing with disparate regulations.

2. Rising drug costs

We spend nearly four times as much for pharmaceutical drugs as other industrialized countries. In fact, this represents the single largest area of overspending compared to Europe, where the government regulates drug prices. While our private insurers can negotiate drug prices with manufacturers, Medicare, representing a large percentage of national drug costs, has not been permitted to do this.

---

24   "6 Reasons Healthcare Is So Expensive in the US," Investopedia, April 27, 2021, https://www.investopedia.com/articles/personal-finance/080615/6-reasons-healthcare-so-expensive-us.asp.

3. Healthcare compensation and human capital

In America, doctors earn far more than their average counterparts in other industrialized countries. For example, a US-based orthopedic surgeon can earn almost twice as much as a similar practitioner in Canada.[25] The more specialized your practice is, the more you stand to gain from practicing in the US. By contrast, using current staff to their highest level of responsibility and authority could be very material to keeping costs down.

4. Hospitals for profit

A third of healthcare costs are related to hospital care. Between 2007 and 2014, prices for inpatient and outpatient hospital care rose far faster than physician prices. As in other areas, charges for surgical procedures in America are much higher than in other countries. In Switzerland or the Netherlands, a typical angioplasty will cost roughly $7,000. Here? Over $32,000.

5. Playing defense

Hospitals and doctors fear lawsuits. So they may practice defensive medicine, which, in turn, can result in an overreliance on testing and scans. Further, the cost of some tests is much greater than in other countries. A CT scan will cost around $100 in Canada and $500 in Australia. Here? $900. While it may be important to be cautious, there is little doubt that this practice contributes to rising costs in the US.

---

25   Tom Blackwell, "Canadian Doctors Still Make Dramatically Less Than US Counterparts: Study," *National Post*, September 14, 2011, https://nationalpost.com/news/canada/canadian-doctors-still-make-dramatically-less-than-u-s-counterparts-study.

6. Inconsistent pricing

Because there aren't set prices for medical services, costs can vary wildly depending on the patient's insurance. During the COVID-19 pandemic, the cost of urgent care and lab tests may have averaged around $1,700, but actual provider charges can range from $240 to $4,500.

THE HEALTH INSURANCE NIGHTMARE

Escalating costs of healthcare are challenging, but SUD patients and their families face their own unique experiences when navigating health insurance and coverage. Greg Williams, the managing director of Third Horizon Strategies and manager of the Alliance for Addiction Payment Reform, knows this firsthand from his experiences as a young man plagued by SUD. He tells his story:

> I got pretty heavily addicted in my adolescence, and my family, after a number of challenging incidences, decided to send me in 2001 to a treatment program that was out of network, out of state. We had coverage for that treatment, at the time they were 80 percent paid for out of network and 20 percent the patient's responsibility. That's how most benefits were structured for out of network care back then.
>
> I had already failed outpatient and overdosed a few times, and after I got there, they called my family on day three and they were like, "The insurance is saying this could be done as an outpatient. He doesn't qualify, he hasn't failed enough." Then my family was like, "Well, he's going to die. We'll figure it out, just keep him." My family was privileged and able to find a path to underwriting the remainder

of what ended up being like a thirty-day stay and then I was placed in a four-month recovery house. I came back home and I've been in recovery ever since. I just celebrated nineteen years.

I was probably a year into recovery and I asked my dad, "Hey, did you ever appeal to the insurance company for the care, because obviously it was medically necessary. It obviously worked. I'm in recovery." And he's like, "Nah, that's a lot of paperwork." I ended up pushing him and he did it. He spent six months, collected the paperwork, filed the appeal and within two weeks they rejected the appeal.

In Connecticut, there were three levels of appeal at the time, so then he did the second level of appeal, where they bring you into the corporate headquarters of the insurance company and you plead your case in front of their internal board. My father was in healthcare and he knew his way around. He walked in and he told my story. I was two years sober at this point. He walked out of that room thinking, "Every single person knew I was right." Two weeks later he gets a rejection notice in his mailbox from the appeal.

So, he went for the third level of appeal, which goes to an independent body at the state agency of insurance. He did that appeal and finally, after over two years since my treatment, they overturned the case and forced the insurance company to pay the claim.

Greg was lucky his family had the resources to cover treatment. Many aren't in that privileged position. Relapse and overdoses can result in frequent ED visits or inpatient admissions where patients incur high healthcare costs. It's a frustrating cycle that may fail patients and strain the system. As Greg sees it, it's just plain bad business.

NOT KEEPING UP

In nearly every other high-income country, people have both become richer over the last three decades and been able to enjoy substantially longer lifespans. But not in the United States. Even as average incomes have risen, much of the economic gains have gone to the affluent—and life expectancy has risen only three years since 1990. There is no other developed country that has suffered such a stark slowdown in lifespans.

—Leonhardt and Serkez, *New York Times*, 2020

Why are insurance companies shooting themselves in the foot by denying care? Since I got into recovery, I haven't been in the ER once, I haven't been in car accidents. I was young and so I wasn't super expensive, but when you start to think about it, it's nonsensical the way that they scrutinized and managed behavioral health benefits.

What we're still buying as payers in addiction treatment doesn't match the nature of the condition. We have this very acute care-centric, fragmented delivery system and that's not anyone's fault, it's how it developed. But if you ask anybody who understands SUDs or read the Surgeon General's report, patients need a care continuum, five years of recovery, in order to get back to the general population.

We've got to start thinking about this as a chronic disease in the frame of diabetes and heart disease.

THE BOTTOM LINE

Our healthcare system is unsustainable in its current form.

Unfortunately, much of this grim reality comes down to money. Spending is driven by utilization (the number of services used) and price (the amount charged per service). An increase in either of these factors results in even higher healthcare costs.

According to the Peter G. Peterson Foundation, we also spend over $800 per person on administrative costs: almost five times more than the average of other wealthy countries and significantly more than we spend on preventive or long-term healthcare.

PRIVATE EQUITY AND TREATMENT

Any conversation about SUD treatment and money should include the role of private equity.

The opioid epidemic spurred investments amounting to billions of dollars by private equity firms who saw an opportunity to build lucrative businesses while ostensibly supporting the public good. Unfortunately, too often, some of these companies weren't offering the most cost-effective services for the largest pool of patients. Why? Because it's easy to make money by repeatedly treating those who continually relapse when there is little accountability for outcomes. Further, investor-owned providers often have direct payment rather than traditional private insurers or Medicare/Medicaid, as those payment rates might fall short of their revenue goals. These strategies have increased insurance costs and put care out of reach for some patients.

While some early investors in this field may have subscribed to this thinking, we expect private equity will ultimately inspire innovation and allow for improvements in the field. Realignment of investments to fuel innovation and drive the outcomes is critical, resulting in a long-term win for the public and private good.

Drew Rothermel, CEO of BRC Healthcare and a leading C-suite executive in the treatment industry, breaks down four different ways investors look at the financial side of treatment, most of which leave the average patient out of the equation.

I would say that there are four buckets of patients and then payment sources for those patients.

First, you have super wealthy folks who are going to elite private facilities. That's $2,000 a day cash. And those programs are very full right now. So that's the first bucket.

The second bucket is the bucket that most private equity was going after. And that bucket was the patient who used some of their own cash for treatment and used their out-of-network benefits for the rest. There's so much competition there that unless you have a brand that allows you to be in that bucket, it's a tough time. Basically, you spend a ton of money on the internet to advertise for patients. Out-of-network insurance was never designed to be a payment strategy, from an insurance company's perspective. When they had a whole industry trying to capitalize on these excess rates for out-of-network, it really hurt the insurance companies and then they really overreacted. So, collecting out-of-network benefits from a treatment center's perspective is complicated. There's an uncertainty as to the timing of the cash flow, which is always something that investors don't like.

The next bucket would be just in-network, where you go to whoever's contracting with your insurance company. If XYZ treatment center is contracted with your insurance, you go there. There's still probably an unmet need there, but it's lower margin, so it's less interesting to private equity.

Last is the publicly funded bucket, which is a hard business.

I would say that private equity has had sporadic results in their access in the business. Some have done really well, some have been total disasters. And I think the one thing that all private equity has gotten smarter about is there's a unique operating culture in this industry from other health-care. And really, there is a limited pool of people who can operate these things. If you don't have one of those people, you're really in trouble.

First of all, I think there needs to be transparent outcomes available, and that has not really happened. And part of it, honestly, is everyone's been lying about their outcomes for so long, and the truth is so much worse than what they've been telling people that they don't really want to get into it. The other thing is, for the longest time, the only outcome that mattered was long term sobriety. But as we know, this is a chronic illness, so people are going to relapse. I mean, that's just a factor of life. So there need to be other measurements.

I think private equity investment in this space has been helpful because they've forced a professionalization of the industry, which hasn't hurt. But I'll tell you, there's a misconception that for-profits are just in it for the money and they're cutting corners. My argument to that would be that, for the solo entrepreneur, they are cutting corners. They don't know what they're doing, they're cutting corners. Once there's fiduciary money behind a facility, that is not the case. But with all the private equity money chasing acquisitions, it has really fueled the growth of the, which I would say in polite company, the recovery entrepreneur. Or, in a more cynical moment, I call it, "Daddy, buy me a rehab so I have a job."

They have to meet the licensing standard. They have to get accredited, but you can hire consultants to get you through that. But once they are accredited, you have the recovering kid of the wealthy family who typically reacts to the pressure of running this kind of business by relapsing a few times. And then, when you look at everyone that works there, they're all twenty-somethings who have no experience or specific skillset to be doing the jobs they're doing. Once you get open, though, there's so much money coming in that even if you didn't know what you're doing, you had the luxury of cashflow to figure it out or to hire some people who are qualified. But the fact of the matter is, people like that can never hire people like me, who are what you need to actually run one of these businesses.

I feel like good people want to be part of good work. The patients do better, the outcomes are better. The patient communities are easier to manage. So it's a win-win all the way around. And at the end of the day, I truly believe that good treatment is the best financial investment. If you do all the right things in this business, you will make the money. You may not make the most money, but you're going to make a lot of money and it's going to be over a long period of time.

Our model is to have that person in our continuum of care for a year. They could spend three, four or five months in BRC and then the rest of the year in the sober living and coaching component and, if they needed access to our psychiatrist or other resources we offer, they can get it during that period of time. So, you shorten the relapse. A relapse can become a couple of days, instead of a couple months. There's a peer community with a lot of pressure to do the right thing.

* * *

As the saying goes, money makes the world go 'round. Obviously, it profoundly affects treatment. Despite all the negative numbers we've shared, the fact of the matter is American healthcare isn't all bad. For example, our technology is so advanced that many rich individuals from other countries choose to have their surgeries performed here. But, again, these are people with the resources to pay for whatever treatment they require.

The overwhelming majority of our own citizens are not in that fortunate situation. While many public facilities allow access to care even without insurance, there are only a limited number of beds to support care. In private insurance settings, policy limits can disrupt care delivery. Patients and families perceive these challenges as barriers that may inhibit them from seeking care. Patients may not know their options; they may not know how to navigate care if they don't have insurance; and they may not understand or appreciate policy limits from insurance. Even if resources were fully available, our system can be hard to use.

Even before the pandemic, our system's limitations on quality outcomes were apparent. The Peterson-KFF Health System Tracker has measured some of these trends and discovered the following painful facts[26]:

➡ We have poorer rates of amenable mortality, as measured by the Healthcare Access and Quality Index.

Mortality amenable to healthcare is a measure of the rates of death considered preventable by timely and effective care. This measure indicates how effectively healthcare is delivered. Unfortunately, America comes in last among comparable countries.

➡ We do significantly worse in terms of years of life lost (YLL).

An alternative to overall mortality rate, premature deaths are measured in years of life lost. We trail comparable countries by a significant margin (12,282 versus 7,764 YLLs in 2017).

26 Nisha Kurani et al., "How Does the Quality of the US Healthcare System Compare to Other Countries?" Peterson-KFF Health System Tracker, August 20, 2020, https://www.healthsystemtracker.org/chart-collection/quality-u-s-healthcare-system-compare-countries/#item-percent-used-emergency-department-for-condition-that-could-have-been-treated-by-a-regular-doctor-2016.

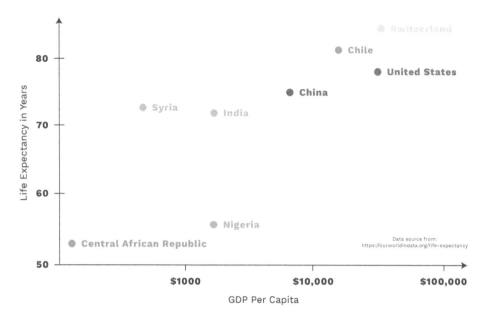

➡ Disease burden is higher here than in comparable countries.

Disability adjusted life years (DALYs) are a measure of disease burden. The rate per 100,000 shows the total number of years lost to disability and premature death. Our DALYs rate is 31 percent higher than the comparable country average.

➡ Hospital admissions for preventable diseases are more frequent in the US.

Hospital admissions for certain chronic diseases like circulatory conditions, asthma, and diabetes increase when preventative care is either not delivered or prioritized. In the US, we have a 37 percent higher rate than in comparable countries for congestive heart failure, asthma, and complications due to diabetes. Given what we've discussed, these numbers may not compare favorably for SUD-related conditions.

➡ We have an overreliance on emergency department use in place of routine doctor visits.

United States vs. Comparable Countries

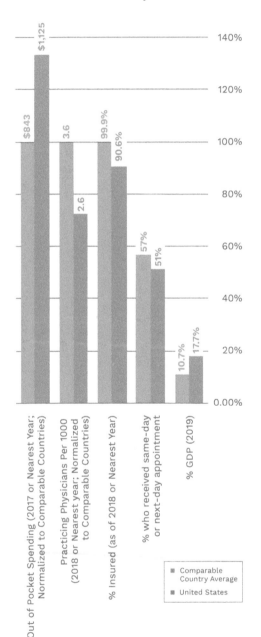

In similar countries, 9 percent of patients visited an ED for nonemergency care, compared with 16 percent of patients in the US. In addition, there are a variety of other comparisons highlighted in the graphic.

These statistics are heavily influenced by the fact that we are not deploying sufficient preventative care to stop unnecessary diseases and deaths even though we are spending considerably more on healthcare than similar countries do.

As demonstrated by Health Tracker, we actually do better on cardiovascular mortality and cancer than others. Interestingly, these are two primary areas where there has been substantial holistic management and evidence-based care, including the development of cancer centers of excellence and thoughtful emergency-response initiatives for heart attack, stroke, and so forth. If we could apply this same type of thinking to SUD patients ... well, keep reading and shortly, you'll see how this could (and should) work.

HIGHER PRICES, HIGHER DISPARITIES

As the healthcare costs continue to rise, health disparities are exacerbated. "There are huge inequalities in this country that often get overlooked ... If you want to observe the problems of poverty and inequality, you don't need to travel all the way to Malawi. You can go to a rural house in America," said Ichiro Kawachi, chair of the Harvard T. H. Chan School of Public Health's Department of Social and Behavioral Sciences. "If you're born a black man in, let's say, New Orleans Parish, your average life expectancy is worse than the male average of countries that are much poorer than America."[27]

America's poor (no matter the race or ethnicity) are sicker than the wealthy. This scenario has played out vividly with the COVID-19 pandemic. Poor communities have become hotspots for COVID transmission, and the death rate has been higher among African Americans than Caucasians. In Michigan, for example, 40 percent of coronavirus deaths have been among Black people even though they make up only 14 percent of the state's population.[28]

The Harvard Gazette identifies three reasons for these health disparities: (1) differences in the frequency of health conditions, (2)

---

27   Alvin Powell, "The Costs of Inequality: Money = Quality Health Care = Longer Life," The Harvard Gazette, February 22, 2016, https://news.harvard.edu/gazette/story/2016/02/money-quality-health-care-longer-life/.

28   Grace A. Noppert, "COVID-19 Is Hitting Black and Poor Communities the Hardest, Underscoring Fault Lines in Access and Care for Those on Margins," The Conversation, April 9, 2020, https://theconversation.com/covid-19-is-hitting-black-and-poor-communities-the-hardest-underscoring-fault-lines-in-access-and-care-for-those-on-margins-135615.

access to care, and (3) variability in insurance coverage.[29] While the federal government has improved the third with the Affordable Care Act (ACA), gaps in the quality and delivery of care remain. These disparities worsen healthcare costs. According to the Kaiser Family Foundation, they contribute to approximately $93 billion in annual excess cost and $42 billion attributable to a loss in work productivity.[30]

Many Americans remain uncovered by health insurance, and numbers are going up, not down: as of 2018, 27.9 million people lacked coverage, an increase of 1.2 million from 2016. That upward trend may continue because of the economic effects of COVID-19, threatening improvements in access to care and overall health following the implementation of the ACA. Some reasons individuals lack coverage include the cost of care being too high, dependency on employers, loss of Medicaid, transitions, or a perceived lack of need for coverage.[31] The uninsured receive less preventative care and are more likely to suffer serious illness or other health problems that could have been mitigated if diagnosed earlier.

OPPORTUNITIES ABOUND

Mental health services are innovators in models of care delivery ... but are laggards in learning from and adopting advances in monitoring and improving the quality of continuing care derived from other chronic disease disciplines.

—Martin Price, *World Psychiatry*, January 19, 2018

29   Colleen Walsh, "COVID-19 Targets Communities of Color," The Harvard Gazette, April 14, 2020, https://news.harvard.edu/gazette/story/2020/04/health-care-disparities-in-the-age-of-coronavirus/.

30   Nambi Ndugga and Samantha Artiga, "Disparities in Health and Health Care: 5 Key Questions and Answers," Kaiser Family Foundation, May 11, 2021, https://www.kff.org/disparities-policy/issue-brief/disparities-in-health-and-health-care-five-key-questions-and-answers/#:~:text=Moreover%2C%20health%20disparities%20are%20costly,losses%20due%20to%20premature%20deaths.

31   Jennifer Tolbert and Kendal Orgera, "Key Facts about the Uninsured Population," Kaiser Family Foundation, November 6, 2020, https://www.kff.org/uninsured/issue-brief/key-facts-about-the-uninsured-population/.

The disparities built into our system have been a significant challenge for behavioral healthcare delivery. In recent years, there have been efforts to compensate for traditional inequities. The US Mental Health Parity Act of 2008 required mental illness treatment to be reimbursed on par with physical illness. The US Affordable Care Act of 2012 was also instrumental, abolishing lifetime and thirty-day limits on inpatient behavioral healthcare. In 2016, the 21st Century Cures Act further clarified the parity goals of the 2008 legislation. Concomitant with legislative changes, there has been an increase in mental health awareness, a decrease in the stigma of behavioral health treatment, and an increase in younger individuals receiving care.

While these efforts are driving improvements, they have only provided a modicum of relief to date and are not a comprehensive solution. A full picture requires evaluation and a plan for the overall cost of care. In the words of famed business expert Peter Drucker, "If you can't measure it, you can't improve it."[32]

Unfortunately, as we discussed before, quantification of behavioral health conditions is a challenge. The substantial fragmentation in the management remains a significant barrier to capturing adequate data. When behavioral health diagnoses lead to physical health concerns, those concerns are siloed and managed separately. For example, if a patient with alcohol use disorder develops cirrhosis, the cirrhosis is managed by a hepatologist. Many patients continue smoking even after the development of lung cancer and receipt of a partial lung resection. While smoking cessation may not have an immediate effect on cancer progression, cessation will reduce the chance of a stroke fairly quickly.

The divide between physical health and behavioral health is probably never as clear as it is when it comes to monitoring disease

---

32   Dave Lavinsky, "The Two Most Important Quotes in Business," Growthink, accessed September 1, 2021, https://www.growthink.com/content/two-most-important-quotes-business.

and quantifying the overall cost of care. Professionals in the behavioral health field are doing amazing boots-on-the-ground work each day by coordinating care across multiple fronts and remaining patient focused. Nevertheless, many opportunities remain in adopting the chronic disease model, tracking outcomes, evaluating total cost of care, and supporting ongoing disease maintenance.

How do we track and trace the costs of treating a patient's SUD needs? We can start by breaking down the five universal elements of care management that have applicability across many conditions, such as hypertension, diabetes, chronic obstructive pulmonary disease, psychosis, epilepsy, and depression.

1. Identification (detection and diagnosis)

2. Engagement (agreement on management plan)

3. Adherence (support for active participation in care)

4. Retention/dropout (keeping patient in the system)

5. Outcome monitoring (reviewing treatment progress and revising if necessary)

This framework narrows the data points that need to be collected to five. If we can successfully collect that data, we can get a handle on where the gaps are and address each care gap. The resulting targeted approach can both improve clinical utility and reduce costs.

Through it all, we must remember the value of preventative care: it's good for the patient, good for the community, and good for the bottom line. Costly care, in turn, not only financially burdens the patient but also negatively impacts the quality and length of their life. We've already discussed how patients may only seek treatment in emergencies. This must change.

When we unlock the actual cost of care, we can improve the care itself. If we track and measure cost for these five data points throughout a patient's journey, we can make informed decisions. We can also prove to key stakeholders that coordinated preventative and proactive treatments can actually lower costs by eliminating much of the need for emergency crisis care.

> We must remember the value of preventative care: it's good for the patient, good for the community, and good for the bottom line.

The CDC currently estimates that the total economic burden of prescription opioid misuse alone in America is *$78.5 billion* a year. That number isn't just about the costs of healthcare and addiction treatment; it also reflects lost productivity and criminal justice involvement. Further, the opioid mortality rate has now outpaced that of the AIDS epidemic at its peak in the early 1990s, before an effective treatment had been formulated.[33] Clearly, how we currently manage SUD does not yet benefit patients or society at large to the extent that it should.

In the next chapter, let's talk about how we can do better.

---

33   Caroline M. Parker et al., "Facing Opioids in the Shadow of the HIV Epidemic," *NEJM*, January 3, 2019, https://www.nejm.org/doi/full/10.1056/NEJMp1813836.

CHAPTER SIX

THE VIRTUE OF VALUE

You treat a disease, you win, you lose. You treat a person, I guarantee you, you'll win, no matter what the outcome.

—PATCH ADAMS

In today's so-called gig economy, about a third of our total workforce gets paid only when they provide a specific service; salaries aren't a part of the deal. That means someone who works through apps such as Uber, TaskRabbit, and Instacart only makes money when they finish the transaction. To earn a living, they must keep taking as much work as possible.

Our healthcare system has many of the traits of a gig economy. It is, in the main, a fee-for-service-based model in which providers and health systems get paid per office visit, lab test, or surgery. Like the Uber drivers and the TaskRabbit repair people, the more they do, the more they make. Therefore, the bottom line for providers depends on this simple precept: *volume, volume, volume.*

Like most things, volume-based care has its upside and downside. On the upside, if patients are using healthcare services for prevention and chronic disease management—which can mitigate poor outcomes and costly complications—volume allows for quality care. If a patient comes through the door routinely and not just when a crisis episode hits them, there are more opportunities to intervene before their condition deteriorates. This type of volume benefits the patient, the provider, and the overall health system, resulting in efficient operations and better outcomes.

There's also the downside of this system—we incentivize the delivery of more services than may be necessary. For example, when a patient is referred to a specialist, they may duplicate tests that the original provider already completed. Further, with SUD care, because of the high utilization of crisis care, a patient could end up being readmitted after having been discharged just three days earlier. The challenge with using volume as a metric is there is a corresponding deemphasis on long-term outcomes. This can obscure which practices are driving better care and which aren't.

In the last chapter, we discussed how healthcare in America is far more costly than in other developed countries. Until a substantial governmental transformation is enacted, we providers can, in the interim, change our approach to care. Instead of being reactive by treating health conditions as they emerge, we can be proactive with prevention or early detection.

Small changes can make a big difference. For example, consider a shift in the approach toward a patient from addressing the day's problem list to prioritizing action needed to mitigate disease progression. Many providers already approach care this way; however, the system is not set up to reimburse them properly for that method of treatment, because providers don't get paid for what *didn't* happen. Accordingly, this limits full adoption of this more holistic approach.

Let's explore a specific example. Consider a forty-six-year-old mother of three who's overweight. Her time is extremely limited.

She holds down two part-time jobs in addition to managing her busy household. She doesn't feel like she has the luxury of exercising or eating "right," and those choices are impacting her long-term health. At each of her last three annual physicals, she has showed a weight gain of around ten pounds and, as a result, she is now borderline obese.

Her primary care physician (PCP), aware that she has a strong family history of diabetes, orders a blood glucose test. The glucose level is normal, and she doesn't have diabetes—*yet*. However, if she continues this trajectory, she has a good chance of developing it. During the physical, the PCP may have counseled her on making lifestyle changes, including offering nutrition guidance—but maybe he didn't. After all, his primary focus was to diagnose, not prevent, and there was really no incentive to do otherwise. Instead, he left things up to his patient. She could engage in making healthier choices in the future—or not. The next step was up to her. And she probably will avoid taking that step and keep on doing what she's doing because she has no idea how to turn things around for her health because of her frantic schedule.

Now let's change the scenario. Suppose (this is a trifle over the top) that same provider was paid $10,000 for every patient she motivated to get their weight down through diet and exercise. If that reward were in place, the provider might do more than advise. She might personally follow up or develop a treatment plan that would be more likely to engage the patient. She may even take the time to talk through a schedule with her and look for ways to empower her to take control of her health. Whatever the case, the takeaway is that if the system rewarded the provider for delivering hands-on, long-term solutions, she may be more motivated to help her patient improve her lifestyle.

Right now, this physician may not have room in her professional schedule to provide that level of care even if she wanted to. She may have had a tough patient appointment before this woman; she could have another one lined up right after her; and she may have an overflowing waiting area filled with patients ready to take up the rest of her day. An alternative might be to reduce her patient load to carve out more time for these efforts; however, she risks damaging the financial performance of the clinic where she works.

As a result, utilization and volume continue to dominate when it comes to this patient's care. The patient comes in; her weight gain is noted; she gets her glucose level tested; and no immediate danger is flagged. The doctor may suggest how she could live healthier, but then the patient gets home, is immediately overwhelmed by the reality of her life, and quickly abandons any thoughts of exercising or improving her diet. Volume-based care simply does not offer her the assistance she needs to ensure her future health.

Brooky Sherwood, an RN and addiction specialist, talks about her experience with her daughter, who's in recovery from SUD, and what she saw lacking in her treatment:

> My daughter was hospitalized at one point because she'd been in a car wreck and the doctors were pretty much refusing to believe she had a problem. And I'm like, "Was she under the influence when she was in the car wreck?" But nobody tested her. It's very unusual that she's alive. It's even more unusual that she didn't go to jail. The number of close calls she had … and the only reason she got away with it was that she was a young, pretty articulate thing. And yes, a white girl.
>
> I think she was still in high school when she had her wisdom teeth out and had her first experience with opioids. She was

prescribed Vicodin. I don't know how long it was before she used IV drugs and was using heroin. She was just on this slippery slide and yeah, I noticed. I noticed she was messed up. I noticed she didn't keep promises. I noticed that she was really sketchy. She was still in school and then moved out and I was still worried. She did detox and rehab multiple times. And then finally, the very last time she went to rehab, she went to Florida to a halfway house and got clean for real.

If I got to run the circus, all programs would be long-term. All rehabs would be long-term and there would be a component of all the things that help a person feel like an important, cared-about contributor to their life and their community. And that's virtually absent in healthcare and it would be expensive to achieve.

> Aligning compensation by outcomes, rather than volume, is more likely to drive better long-term healthcare, as promulgated by *value-based models.*

Aligning compensation by outcomes, rather than volume, is more likely to drive better long-term healthcare, as promulgated by *value-based models.*

Advocating for Value-Based Care

Value-Based Care, with the assumption that value is governed by quality divided by cost, provides higher efficacy and can drive improved outcomes. However, the transition to value-based care is challenging and slow.

$$\text{Value} = \frac{\text{Quality}}{\text{Cost}}$$

The complexity of our system is one of the largest barriers to this evolution. Patients often report that they feel left to their own devices and are required to navigate their own care through a network of providers and insurance company red tape. Patients may see multiple doctors, specialists, and surgeons who often may not communicate effectively with each other or don't have access to the patient's data. This fragmentation can be mirrored in insurance coverage. Multiple payers may work within one geographic area and even a single individual may have primary, secondary, and tertiary coverage.

A second barrier is that no one "owner" drives the deliverables we are hoping to achieve. Individual care providers may not be aligned on the same treatment steps. The inaccessibility of aggregated data limits how deeply we can assess a patient's overall condition. Because the system is a fee-for-service model, physician care is siloed and the providers aren't empowered or incentivized to create technological solutions for care coordination to maintain consistency in care. Mistakes get made; services get duplicated; and one hand doesn't know what the other is doing.

By contrast, value-based care programs are specifically designed to drive down costs and improve overall health. Providers are financially rewarded for being proactive about patient care and outcomes. They're encouraged to engage with patients and customize care to each one's specific circumstances. They're motivated to invest in new technology, evaluate processes and performance, and keep multiple providers in alignment on a patient's care. In short, value-based care programs promote a unified team approach to a patient's medical needs. Costs are lowered, and patient-care quality is lifted. It's a win-win.

CARE FRAGMENTATION

The US healthcare system suffers from high costs that do not yield commensurately high levels of quality. Although there are many competing explanations for this inefficiency, one area of relatively broad consensus is care fragmentation. According to the fragmentation hypothesis, care delivery too often involves multiple providers and organizations with no single entity effectively coordinating different aspects of care. Poor coordination across providers may lead to suboptimal care, including important healthcare issues being inadequately addressed, poor patient outcomes, and unnecessary or even harmful services that ultimately both raise costs and degrade quality.

–Frandsen et al., *American Journal of Managed Care*, May 2015

At the moment, there is agreement among many healthcare professionals that this transition to value-based care needs to happen. In select care segments, there have been successful launches of this type of work. For example, the Outcome and Assessment Information Set (OASIS) data collected by home-care providers successfully supports the clinical-care delivery and reimbursement for certain CMS recipients requiring home care. But while some parts of the country are switching over to this model (Vermont, for example, is ahead of much of the nation in this effort), most are not. One survey shows that fee-for-service models currently account for roughly 75 percent of providers' reimbursements, with 25 percent coming from value-based care. In that same survey, nearly half the respondents, who are clinical leaders, clinicians, and healthcare-company executives, say value-based contracts significantly improve the quality of care as well as significantly lower the cost of care.[34]

So if value-based care can accomplish these two critical goals, why isn't it more widely adopted?

One reason is our system as a whole is stumped on *how* to make the transition. Second, not everyone is completely convinced. According to that same survey, over half of healthcare professionals still aren't sure about value-based care. They're not sure they can trust it. Before they're ready to commit to changing systems, they (not unfairly) need to be confident this change will bring better outcomes. As we transition to a value-based system, we will be accountable for outcomes and driving more cost-efficient and coordinated services. Bridging this gap may be even greater with behavioral health conditions, where regulations and infrastructure limit transparency: a field in which there is little consensus on outcomes in the behavioral health space, difficulty in retrieving robust data, and limited integration into costly physical-health-related sequelae. As such, most of behavioral health remains in the fee-for-service-based paradigm.

As promised, we hope to shed light on areas that can transform care for SUD patients. We strongly believe that a value-based care model is one of these necessary ingredients for strengthening care in this space. This model will extend beyond the current revolving-door fee-for-service system in identifying crucial factors that matter the

---

34   Thomas W. Feeley and Namita Seth Mohta, "Transitioning Payment Models: Fee-for-Service to Value-Based Care," NEJM Catalyst Insights Report, November 2018, https://www.optum.com/content/dam/optum3/optum/en/resources/publications/NEJM_Optum_Transitioning_Payment_Models_2018.pdf.

most: outcomes, costs, safety indicators, patient-experience indicators, and process measures. We hope that by highlighting just how well this model can work we can help drive adoption and policy changes.

HOW COORDINATED CARE CAN UP OUR GAME

Let's start with what should be a hallmark of value-based care and SUD treatment: coordinated patient care. Coordinated care can produce better results and lower costs.

A 2015 study found that insufficient care coordination increases the average costs of chronic disease management by more than $4,500 and fails to improve patients' adherence to recommended protocols.[35] Those who received services from multiple providers were more likely to experience treatment gaps, resulting in high-cost, preventable emergency room visits.

Care coordination is especially relevant in SUD care due to the high prevalence of comorbidities and disease sequelae. For example, we've seen an unprecedented rise in certain bacterial (e.g., *Staphylococcus aureus*) and viral (e.g., HIV and hepatitis) infections in association with intravenous opioid use.[36]

Further, patients' care needs span both the outpatient and inpatient settings given the reliance on crisis care and the corresponding chronic-care management needs, such as treatment-related care and management of disease sequelae. This combination makes care susceptible to high-cost outcomes.

Acute care requires urgent attention and quick treatment and is the result of a single cause. In contrast, chronic-care problems

---

35   Brigham R. Frandsen et al., "Care Fragmentation, Quality, and Costs among Chronically Ill Patients," *American Journal of Managed Care*, May 2015, https://www.ajmc.com/journals/issue/2015/2015-vol21-n5/care-fragmentation-quality-costs-among-chronically-ill-patients?p=3.

36   Sara Reardon, "The US Opioid Epidemic Is Driving a Spike in Infectious Diseases," *Nature*, June 28, 2019, https://www.nature.com/articles/d41586-019-02019-3.

are slower to develop, last longer, and stem from a variety of causes, some of which occur a number of years before symptoms are evident. Well-coordinated care is essential to these kinds of cases, requiring a new paradigm that both encompasses longitudinal care and unplanned crisis-care episodes.

The particularly critical shortfalls in poorly coordinated care rest in the *transition to care*: the movement of patients between locations, providers, or level of care as conditions and treatment needs evolve. When the transition is handled well, medical errors are prevented, issues are detected early enough to successfully intervene, unnecessary hospitalizations and readmissions are prevented, and duplicate services are eliminated. To create efficient transitions of care, there must be a comprehensive care plan in place, a network of practitioners who receive up-to-date information about the patient, and possibly a technology infrastructure that simplifies the solution. While not to detract from the importance of care coordination on patient health, the lack of this type of coordination has a substantial financial impact as well. For example, from a 2011 report: "… poorly coordinated transitions from the hospital to other care settings cost an estimated $12 billion to $44 billion per year and often result in adverse health outcomes (e.g., injuries related to medication errors, post medical procedure complications, infections, falls)."[37]

These cost increases are driven by the fact that no single provider has a global view of a patient's clinical needs. In these settings, gaps in care or duplicity of services arise to the detriment of both the patient and the system as a whole. While many models have advocated for a central "quarterback" role for the primary care provider, these providers may not have the time, visibility, or specialized knowledge

---

37   Janice L. Clarke et al., "An Innovative Approach to Health Care Delivery for Patients with Chronic Conditions," *Population Health Management*, February 1, 2017, https://www.ncbi.nlm.nih.gov/pmc/articles/PMC5278805/.

to identify gaps in care or even repeated tests and services. Since behavioral health services have been managed independently from physical health needs for decades, this integration is particularly challenging in conditions or diseases that span both domains, as seen with SUD.

In addition to silos and fragmentation in care delivery, the billing coding system may fragment the process further. For example, we may code for a disease in one care setting but code a very different diagnosis in another. Getting highly technical for a moment: consider a patient in treatment for chronic back pain with opioids who may receive an ICD-10 diagnosis code of M54.5. However, if this individual requires emergency care for a paralytic ileus that is likely due to his opioid treatment, it will be coded as K56.0. Very few providers or health systems would link these two episodes based on the ICD-10 codes alone. These connections could be readily addressed by digital data gathering.

To fully leverage well-coded data, centralized and integrated health management is necessary. As elaborated in a February 2018 article in *World Psychiatry*, Martin Prince shares his vision of the use of innovation in the mental health space: "Smartphones or tablets, linked by mobile data to cloud servers, can promote the collection, aggregation, timely analysis and use of health management information systems data. After detection of a condition requiring continuing care, the app would generate a bespoke care pathway with follow-up appointments, and prompted actions and assessments (attendance, adherence, and outcome monitoring) to be carried out on each occasion. These basic health management information systems generate an electronic medical record for any healthcare professional providing care (promoting information and provider continuity), and a patient registry to track patients' progress."

The strength of these systems is the use of data to risk-stratify patients, adjust treatment protocols, and manage patient care in real time.

BRINGING VALUE TO THE BEHAVIORAL HEALTH ARENA

As behavioral health issues tend to be at the foundation of those with SUD, we want to recognize how value-based care can improve the treatment of behavioral health patients. We've identified five main points of progress that will take place with this kind of system's adoption.

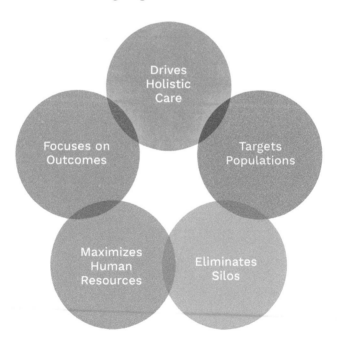

Why a Value-Based Care-Delivery System Is Needed

- Drives Holistic Care
- Targets Populations
- Eliminates Silos
- Maximizes Human Resources
- Focuses on Outcomes

CHAPTER SIX: THE VIRTUE OF VALUE

1. Focuses on outcomes

Behavioral health treatment has traditionally placed a significant focus on the provision of individualized care in this country. Using a strictly individualized approach may compromise one's ability to fully leverage a standardized, evidence-based approach. Having a value-based approach in place forces the conversation on choosing care delivery that has a positive impact that is substantiated through data.

2. Drives holistic care

The behavioral health field has successfully leveraged community resources to support care delivery. Behavioral healthcare delivery also places an important emphasis on the whole person. The value-based approach can place a higher premium on this holistic approach and use of community resources. It can also place a higher priority on the SAoH, which will help these patients and positively influence the cost of care.

3. Targets populations

High-risk patients are often the costliest to treat, and SUD patients are often among the highest-risk, most-complex patients. Because the value-based model places emphasis on addressing patients in high-risk groups, providers would have a stronger chance of materially impacting the health of this population and potentially lowering the overall cost of care.

4. Eliminates silos

Behavioral- and physical-health-delivery models have operated independently for too long. There have been

> Behavioral- and physical-health-delivery models have operated independently for too long.

significant efforts in recent years to integrate these two fields; however, expediency is needed to drive better overall care and outcomes and to reduce cost. A value-based model would motivate a rapid alignment.

5. Maximizes human resources

The behavioral health model effectively leverages all types of providers at various levels of training; this is somewhat distinct from allopathic medicine, where there can often be a higher reliance on MDs and nurse practitioners. An optimized value-based care delivery would support providers practicing at their highest ability.

These five points help provide the why for adopting a value-based model. The sticky part is still the how. There remains substantial ambiguity on how to make this transition, but a few institutional pathways can be used to trigger change.

How to Facilitate a Value-Based Care Delivery System

➡ Thought leadership

We must be disciplined in driving evidence-based work. When that avenue is not available, we should still leverage expertise for guidelines and guidance. Without defining success metrics and putting stakes in the ground, this field will progress slowly, in a siloed manner and we will remain uninformed about best practices. Data can make the difference.

➡ Automation

Our country has demonstrated great skill in automating processes and even jobs. We should extend these successes to the fullest measure within behavioral health. In concert with greater standardization of evidence-based work, we can automate and drive optimal care through improved care delivery and expanded operational effort. This work can support care coordination efforts, smooth out transitions of care, and allow for reduced costs. Unfortunately, automation is only as good as its ability to be adopted. While we often hear providers say they do not want to introduce new technology, they have expressed significant interest in integrating features with current systems.

➡ Risk stratification

The use of analytics, evidence-based work, and automation can allow risk stratification and the creation of assigned risk scores for patients. This will help us identify populations that are complex and require more attention than others.

➡ Patient engagement

The US has always placed individuality at a premium. This can be used to empower patients in their own care through direct-to-patient initiatives, easy access to quality information, and decision-making support. This approach is imperative in behavioral health, where we ask patients to commit to important lifestyle and health behavioral changes.

The Institutional Achievement Index

We've discussed the theoretical advantages of value-based care. Let's now explore what a practical value-based care system could look like.

We authors first became interested in maturity indices after seeing models developed by the nonprofit Healthcare Information and Management Systems Society, which is dedicated to improving the quality, safety, cost-effectiveness, and access of healthcare. Their models are meant to offer, in the organization's words, "strategic pathways that successfully advance key areas of provider maturity, including infrastructure, analytics, coordination of care, clinical documentation, and supply chain infrastructure,"[38] precisely the kind of outcomes we'd like to see for SUD patients and patients who have opioids as part of their treatment.

We developed a maturity index entitled the Institutional Achievement Index (or IAI) and conceived of it as a road map for healthcare organizations such as treatment centers, health systems, and other organizations that are dealing with the complexity of coordinating care for the behavioral population. Our aim is to improve processes while lowering costs and improving care. The elements within this model are a product of an extensive literature review and many conversations with providers, administrators, and treatment staff across the US. Some of the early modeling were expanded upon and influenced by work done by the Substance Abuse and Mental Health Services Administration (SAMHSA). By providing a concrete set of definitions of success and pathway for progress for organizations, the IAI could improve the management of opioid patients. While we provide an introduction here, we will complete the road

---

38 "Who We Are," HIMSS, accessed September 1, 2021, https://www.himssanalytics.org/about.

map to success in chapter 9 with specific tools on how to assess, implement, and measure your own organization's progress.

The index relies upon a basic six-level progression:

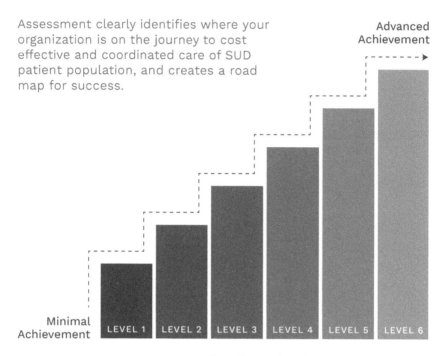

Assessment clearly identifies where your organization is on the journey to cost effective and coordinated care of SUD patient population, and creates a road map for success.

Advanced Achievement

Minimal Achievement

LEVEL 1   LEVEL 2   LEVEL 3   LEVEL 4   LEVEL 5   LEVEL 6

Core Competencies

The process includes assessment questions to define where one stands along the continuum and maps to particular criteria for each level. A summative report can be generated after defining these levels (see material presented at the end of this book).

These assessments ultimately provide detailed explanations of how organizations can progress from one level to the next.

SUD Institutional Achievement Index

Core Competencies	Level 1	Level 2	Level 3	Level 4	Level 5	Level 6
Collaborative stewardship	Minimal or no collaboration or leadership in a fee-for-service health payment model	Establishment of leadership with nascent collaboration in a fee-for-service health payment model	Engaged collaboration and leadership support in a fee-for-service health payment model without effective mechanisms to monitor impact and progress	Leadership and collaboration with the implementation of programmatic performance indicators and consideration of a value-based care payment model	Engaged leadership and/or governance monitoring collaborative impact with transitioning to value-based care payment system	Ongoing, monitored progress demonstrating effective leadership and collaboration within a value-based care payment system
Evidence-based care	Holistic management of Substance Use patients, including social aspects of health, is not achieved. Little to no standard protocols or identification of potential care gaps exist.	Care delivery is focused on the current episode of care with increased recognition of the importance of downstream clinical outcomes. Initial commitment of resources with little to no standard protocols or visibility to potential care gaps	Care delivery has an increased focus on employment of best practice standards with identification of disease sequelae and comorbidities in addition to the active management of patient. Resources are being developed for standard protocols or visibility to emerging care gaps	Care delivery supports best practices with the identification of disease sequelae and comorbidities. Committed resources and standard protocols are in development. Care gaps are recognized but only addressed in a limited way	The organization has developed a holistic care model with adoption of best practices and emerging mechanisms to identify comorbidities and disease sequelae. There is a commitment of adequate resources, standard protocols and recognition of care gaps	There is an organization wide commitment to best practice standards and mechanisms to identify disease comorbidities and sequelae. Fully integrated resources and standard protocols are available and integrated across all care transitions
Chronic care management	No significant adoption of chronic care management model	Early recognition of SUD as a chronic disease model with appreciate of care continuum	Recognition of chronic care model with developing standard resources focused on Substance Use Disorders	Adoption of chronic care model with developing standardized resources across care continuum including prevention, pain management and Substance Use Disorders	Adoption of chronic care model with increasing standardization and focus on prevention and early diagnosis efforts	System-wide adoption of chronic disease model with prioritization on prevention and established standards of care
Patient engagement	Minimal patient/family engagement outside of traditional care models	Initial development of mechanisms to engage patients/families.	Patient engagement strategies are being deployed with an active development of processes to improve patient care or experience. Families are not directly engaged outside of traditional clinical care model	Patient engagement strategies are actively deployed with an evolving consideration of the patient's family and/or community involvement in the patient's care	Patients are actively engaged in their own care with increasing involvement of family and/or community	Patients, families and/or community are actively engaged in care with patients driving continued improvements in care for themselves and others

Strategies such as those outlined in the maturity index help support a much-needed paradigm shift.

If we can create a value-based care delivery model, we can address the most complex, highest-cost patients first. This approach may cause a reversal of our current approach, in line with the famous Bible verse, "The last shall be first and the first last."[39] This intent would reduce complexity and keep costs down. Value-based care also aligns well with patient-centered care and the patient's best interests. In other words, finances are an element of the maturity index but are not the primary rationale for its adoption. Nonetheless, one of the factors of success in this model is acknowledging the role of aligning financial models into the organizational structure to support care.

Because the IAI is designed to give healthcare organizations targets for collaboration and competency, it creates an innovative system-wide approach to supporting patients. Positive global change is the desired result: we must reduce the variation in care seen nationally and also within specific health systems, treatment centers or programs, or even a single provider practice.

By tracking a patient with a specific issue and correlating their case with those of similar patients, we can anticipate comorbidities that might evolve and intervene to help the patient avoid them.

---

39   Matt. 20:16. (King James Version).

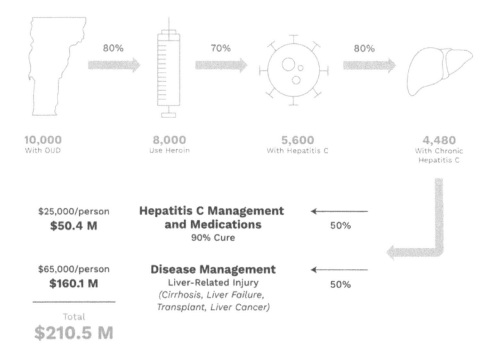

10,000
With OUD

8,000
Use Heroin

5,600
With Hepatitis C

4,480
With Chronic
Hepatitis C

$25,000/person	**Hepatitis C Management**		
$50.4 M	**and Medications**	←	
	90% Cure	50%	

$65,000/person	**Disease Management**	←	
$160.1 M	Liver-Related Injury	50%	
	(Cirrhosis, Liver Failure,		
	Transplant, Liver Cancer)		

Total

$210.5 M

For example, many SUD patients may contract hepatitis C. As outlined in the graphic, we can see the financial cost of that scenario in just the state of Vermont.

If we estimate there are about ten thousand people with OUD in that state, statistically, about 80 percent (or eight thousand) of them will use heroin. Seventy percent of those who use heroin will have hepatitis C exposure. About 80 percent of those will develop chronic hepatitis C. Half of those will seek treatment, and medication will cure roughly 90 percent of this group.

Besides the health risks, hepatitis C itself is expensive, averaging $25,000 per person, for a total cost of $50.4 million. However, those who choose not to seek help to manage their hepatitis C may develop liver-related pathology, and *that* will end up costing $65,000 per person, totaling $160.1 million.

If we're able to reduce the heroin exposure in just two hundred Vermonters—you read that right, two hundred, with no extra zeros—we can save $5.2 million. And, importantly, the health of those two hundred people will benefit greatly.

Example #2: Overdose Cost in VT

Here's one more example of how we can improve on results if we would just change up our approach to treatment. Using those 10,000 Vermonters with OUD as our base point again, we can see approximately 2,000 of them will show up in an ED for urgent care. Some 1,400 of them will require EMS. Of those who end up in an ED, 860 will receive inpatient care, 400 will have a Narcan reversal and leave, and 250 people will go into the ICU. Of the original 2,000 who did go to the ED, 210 will end up back there again in a year and 110 will die of overdoses.

Besides the brutal blows to personal health and the tragic loss of human life that will result from this downward spiral, total hospital costs will exceed *$16 million.*

If we intervene early and effectively with coordinated care, before more serious health issues manifest, we can avoid these negative outcomes. This effort begins with tracking costs of care, as we did in Vermont, so we can identify gaps in ongoing care and address them. All this will give us a big assist in transitioning from a volume-based care model to a value-based care model—because we can prove savings to healthcare payers and persuade them to endorse alternative care protocols.

What You Can Do

We recognize that it takes time and tremendous effort to modify our system so that it reflects a value-based mindset. So—what do you do if you're an individual provider who wants to see value-based care implemented but you feel like you're fighting a battle nobody wants you to win?

Here are a few suggestions.

➡ Advocate.

Promote value-based and population-health-based concepts within your own institution through existing channels—such as committees, interdisciplinary committees, grand rounds, and C-suite discussions.

➡ Partner with payers.

Payers may seem like they are on the sidelines in these types of discussions, but obviously, they retain a lot of power. Payers are always looking for new solutions to rising costs—and if one of those solutions is proven, they will pay for it. Because value-based care has the potential to lower costs, they are increasingly open to building opportunities to test out these types of efforts. Gaining their support could help convince your own organization to get on board.

➡ Work within your own practice.

Leverage your own staff creatively in care, and find ways to employ lower-cost staff as much as possible. Demonstrate efficiency in what you do, and the results will attract attention.

➡ Pick your battles.

Rome wasn't built in a day. Shifting our healthcare system to a value-based model will take time and effort. With that in mind, just pick a few improvement projects and prioritize those. Approach them in an evidence-based manner and showcase the results of these efforts to others.

➡ Adopt technology that will help you in your work.

Data collection is key to providing strong, coordinated care. Think about what you can use to keep your patient data up to date and ready to relay to another provider, should it be necessary.

➡ Ask the patients what they need.

Your patients, particularly those who have been on the journey for some time, can have incredible insights into their care and their own needs. Engage, solicit, and respond to the feedback they provide. They have a wealth of ideas to offer. But be prepared to mobilize in response to patients' requests—especially in a value-based care model.

➡ Work with others.

Along those same lines, think about how you can work more closely with other practitioners to serve your patients better. How can you better integrate their care with your own toward a patient's best interests? Think outside the box, and you'll get there. Consider this discussion with Miro Weinberger, the mayor of Burlington, Vermont. He articulates the value of collaboration in Burlington's model.

> Burlington had come a long way on improving access, we'd done a lot of work making it much easier and really improving our systems for inducing people into medically assisted treatment. We had lowered a lot of the barriers to people getting into treatment. We eliminated this waiting list that had plagued the community for years for access to treatment. And then we found that wasn't good enough, that even without a waiting list there was still a wait, people waiting fourteen to seventeen days before getting their first doses of medicine. And so we attacked that. We created these nodes that were essentially immediate access points into our "hub and spoke" system, in our prisons, our emergency room here in Burlington, and at our needle exchange/safe recovery where people would basically have an opportunity to immediately, as soon as they agreed to treatment, get their first doses of the medicine.

> The city actually doesn't have its own health department. We don't have direct responsibility for many of these services. But what we did do is we created this effort, we call it "Community Stat," which is a monthly meeting based on the city stat principles of being focused on data, being focused on rapid deployment of resources, relentless follow-up and other effective tactics. We applied that model to the opioids, and it has been used for many things from law enforcement to all sorts of different municipal challenges. We applied it to this multi-agency coordinating effort.

We'd had this waiting list for years. Within six months of when we started talking at "Community Stat," the waiting list was gone. You add all this up, and yes, I think it was one of the most robust local efforts to combat the opioid epidemic in the country. And in the first three years of the history of that effort, county opioid deaths dropped 50% and stayed down there from 2017 to '18 and then '18 to '19.

But we still were having a significant number of deaths. These people are often struck down in the prime of life, they're parents, they're effective workers, they have loving siblings. The deaths are just so tragic. So I thought we needed to keep going with this. What I realized and my colleagues realized is, we had this huge push to get people into treatment, but there had been very little focus on retention and keeping people in treatment.

So we really tried to shift the focus to retention, and I think that was the right instinct. And I think that is where we have made substantial improvements to our systems. But we definitely got knocked off course on that by the arrival just a few months later, in March, of the coronavirus. And the whole world changed.

My great hope is we could eventually have some kind of coordinated entry system like we have for the way we serve the homeless population here now. It's like if someone comes in, it doesn't matter which part of the system someone enters homelessness, they are tracked in a coordinated way that all the agencies working with the homeless population have access to and share information. That, to me, is clearly what we should have for the opioid epidemic.

The mayor is right—and it's time we changed that fact. That's why we've written this book, and that's why we've been working hard on a comprehensive approach to treating BH/SUD patients, which we're about to share.

* * *

Changes to our healthcare system over the years have generally fixated on addressing the ever-increasing costs, with the Affordable Care Act being the latest and most substantial attempt to rein them in. But it's time we go beyond the dollars and cents and look at our actual model of care delivery. It's clear that regardless of the payment model, healthcare needs to shift its focus from being transactional to being more impactful. This need is urgent because we continue to face new and increasingly overpowering health challenges. Whether it's the COVID-19 pandemic or the opioid crisis, we have no time to waste on less results-oriented strategies. Outcomes need to be our focus and priority.

Ultimately, transitioning to a value-based model is going to reduce both the cost to and risk for consumers, making treatment more accessible and affordable. It will also help care teams and clinical institutions provide more coordinated and on-target treatments. In the next chapter, we'll explore in greater details the difficulties inherent in our current system—and how we can make care more equitable for all concerned.

CHAPTER SEVEN

THE FIGHT FOR EQUITY

*The essence of global health equity is the idea that something
so precious as health might be viewed as a right.*

—PAUL FARMER

In the last chapter, we discussed the problem with our current fragmented health system. Having a revolving door of patients going in and out of different provider offices for different issues means their health concerns are not holistically addressed over the long haul, particularly when specialists come into play. One hand frequently doesn't know what the other is doing, and long-term solutions to long-term conditions are sadly lacking in many cases.

Nowhere is that distressing fact more apparent than when it comes to those grappling with SUD and behavioral health. Studies show that only 10 percent of those with SUD are getting treatment.

While the past few years have seen substantial governmental and health system commitments to infrastructure, the acceleration of the mental health crisis in concert with the COVID-19 pandemic portends further barriers lie ahead. As we've noted, stigma prevents many from seeking help. They worry that if they admit to their condition, they will be judged harshly by families, friends, and employers. But stigma isn't the whole story.

Our system simply isn't set up to help patients promote sustainable recovery. There are barriers to effective care that leave many out in the cold and that, unfortunately, can too often be a death sentence. We must break down those barriers to restore *equity* to medical care. We believe no other population is this big and no other disease has greater priority or urgency.

Let's unpack these inequities to determine how to promote sustainable recovery and well-being in all our patients.

SUD INEQUITIES

In 2015, an estimated 2.3 million people aged twelve or older who needed substance use treatment received treatment at a specialty facility in the past year. This number represents 0.9 percent of all people aged twelve or older and 10.8 percent of the 21.7 million people who needed substance use treatment.

—Lipari et al., CBHSQ Report, 2016, SAMHSA

What's Behind Patient Inequities

It all begins, as you might have guessed, with the *cost of care*.

Despite strides with the Affordable Care Act, affordability, especially for those with limited means, remains a challenge. In the words of Brooky Sherwood, an RN who has been working with SUD patients for years,

In general, the system, we're kind of like running around with Band-Aids on a huge problem. I don't know that we can do a lot better than that right now. A lot of it is the way that healthcare is delivered in the US and insurance companies and what gets paid for. One of the things that drives me wild is all of my Vermont Medicaid patients get everything paid for until they're doing really well and they have a decent job and then, suddenly, they're not on Vermont Medicaid anymore. And then, whoa, boy, it becomes much more difficult. And I'm like, wait a minute, but they're doing so well. Shouldn't we help with that?

With that large fact in mind, we need to create a cost model that does make lifelong treatment feasible for all.

The Mental Health Parity and Addiction Equity Act, passed in 2008, has made strides in addressing the disparity in care between the affluent and the average American. This has led to a limited approach toward integrating behavioral health issues with primary care but, to date, has had only a relatively small impact on the opioid crisis.

As we await full-service integration for behavioral health and physical-health needs, treatment centers can operate rather independently. And many have positioned themselves as luxury treatment programs, designed for the wealthy. Luxury rehab centers can afford to advertise heavily throughout all types of media because of the exorbitant rates they charge. At The Meadows in Arizona, for example, it costs almost $55,000 for a forty-five-day stay. The ultimate example of this phenomenon is perhaps Paracelsus Recovery in Zurich, Switzerland, where a one-week "executive detox" costs over US$100,000![40] Based on a 2006 *Forbes* report, these centers typically

---

40   Max Daly, "Inside the Drug Rehab for the World's Super Rich," *Vice*, December 6, 2019, https://www.vice.com/en_us/article/mbm8mp/where-super-rich-go-rehab-paracelsus.

range between $14,000 and $40,000 per month, with insurance coverage only supporting a few hundred dollars. While some have argued that the growing prominence of these types of centers may help support antistigma efforts, they are not equitable. And while there is no reliable data to suggest that cost equates with outcomes, it is clear that most patients have a more limited repertoire of programs to choose from.

In our current shortage of mental healthcare professionals, where do our patients go?

To date, many patients access care through the ED. In some cases, patients may be identified as having a clear medical need by employers or family members. But what if we could leverage the existing medical care infrastructure to better support our SUD? With increasing investments in buprenorphine-based MAT therapies in outpatient primary care offices, many governments and institutions are committing substantial resources to do just that.

> In our current shortage of mental healthcare professionals, where do our patients go?

However, most traditional medical providers aren't sufficiently equipped to treat SUD patients. From Kaiser Health News:

Jonathan Goodman can recall most of the lectures he's attended at the Stanford University School of Medicine. He can recite detailed instructions given more than a year ago about how to conduct a physical.

But at the end of his second year, the twenty-seven-year-old MD-PhD student could not remember any class dedicated to addiction medicine. Then he recalled skipping class months earlier. Reviewing his syllabus, he realized he had missed the sole lecture dedicated to that topic.

"I wasn't tested on it," Goodman said, with a note of surprise.[41]

He shouldn't be surprised. Even in the middle of a huge opioid addiction crisis, physicians are alarmingly undertrained in SUD treatment. Within the past five years or so, there has been a recognition of this huge gap in addiction medicine education and some scattered efforts to address it in medical schools and residency programs, but those efforts can be spotty, with minimal standardization.

EDUCATION GAP

Compounding the profound gap between the need for addiction treatment and the receipt of such care is the enormous gulf between the knowledge available about addiction and its prevention and treatment and the education and training received by those who provide or should provide care.

—CASA Columbia Study, 2012

What's shocking is that according to a Columbia University report, most individuals experiencing SUD in the US do not receive any treatment from a physician. Alarmingly, addiction care is often provided by people without the medical or mental healthcare training required to effectively deliver evidence-based interventions.[42] As for

---

41   Natalie Jacewicz, "Teaching Future Doctors About Addiction," Kaiser Health News, August 2, 2016, https://khn.org/news/teaching-future-doctors-about-addiction/.

42   "Addiction Medicine: Closing the Gap between Science and Practice," The National Center on Addiction and Substance Abuse at Columbia University, June 2012.

the medical community itself, the same study showed that most medical professionals who should be providing addiction treatment are not sufficiently trained to diagnose or treat it and that 94 percent of US physicians did not include SUD among the five diagnoses they offered when presented with symptoms of alcohol abuse.

There is no question that most providers have a lot on their plate. They are notoriously overwhelmed due to the volume-based nature of their business model, and that undermines their ability to attend to individual patients and deliver value, especially in this population that often requires extensive care and support structures outside standard care delivery. The system is designed to motivate them to chase transactions, not holistic health approaches to SUDs. Further, providers may not have the time to educate themselves about those approaches.

We must create an approach for them that is simple and easily implemented. Providers already must stay on top of a myriad of chronic illnesses; they may not have extra bandwidth to address the full complexity of many SUD patients' needs. One approach that shows promise is the addiction recovery medical home model, which combines a coordinated treatment and recovery plan with a payment model, quality metrics, a care recovery team, and a support network.

Keeping Medical Providers in the Picture

Given the barriers to education and the possible alternative strategies of treatment programs that have historically been the mainstay of care, why try to involve providers through traditional medical care delivery at all?

The answer is simple: medical care providers can help break down the barriers to care and help create an equitable treatment model.

While they may not be the first line of care accessed by patients, what if they could be leveraged that way?

Medical care providers may be much easier for patients to access than specialty care centers. They are generally geographically dispersed and ubiquitous. Many primary care offices are designed to receive walk-ins, and some patients may have preexisting relationships. ED providers, already seeing patients in acute-care episodes, may be able to support transitions and warm handoffs. Some patients may see their primary care physicians often enough that the provider can help drive long-term recovery and care—if there is a road map in place the doctor can follow.

Further, when it comes to cost, most health insurance policies make primary care treatments relatively affordable. If PCPs could be given the resources to deliver the kind of long-term care we consider essential, it would go a long way toward correcting the financial inequities that plague the system and keep patients from getting the care they need.

The question then becomes, How can we improve medical care when it comes to SUD patients? The key is to develop and agree upon a road map and resources that will allow outpatient providers to track patients' progress through data-driven protocols and that can easily be shared with other providers when necessary. This will help an overwhelmed provider drive a holistic approach to care and eliminate the challenge of creating individualized treatment plans for every new patient. Real-time dashboards can enable providers to review protocols of care so that they can quickly access the tools and information they need to manage addiction as a chronic illness.

This is a change that needs to happen enterprise-wide across healthcare institutions. Better outcomes require sufficient care coordination that spans providers, other enterprise efforts, treatment centers, and available community resources. And that brings us to our next recommendation.

Centers of Excellence

To provide the most holistic care possible, we need to make that care more comprehensive. One approach that has been used across other diseases and conditions is to develop centers of excellence dedicated to treatment.

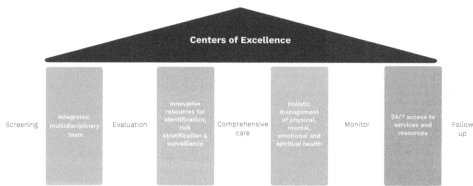

Formally defined, a center of excellence is "a program within a healthcare institution which supplies an exceptionally high concentration of expertise and related resources centered on a particular area of medicine, delivering associated care in a comprehensive, interdisciplinary fashion to afford the best patient outcomes possible."[43] Since there is no *official* definition of centers of excellence, with the exception of a few credentialing programs for specific services, the term is applied broadly and inconsistently.

---

43   James K. Elrod and John L. Fortenberry, Jr., "Centers of Excellence in Healthcare Institutions: What They Are and How to Assemble Them," *BMC Health Services Research*, 2017.

Nonetheless, health professionals generally agree that a center of excellence typically provides a comprehensive package of services aimed at treating a specific disease. Prominent examples of conditions with centers of excellence include bariatric surgery services, stroke care, and breast care. This focus creates an elevated level of expertise that serves those suffering from the targeted condition at a higher level.

That's precisely what we're after for our patients.

Unfortunately, while there are many centers of excellence dedicated to other chronic diseases, those dedicated to behavioral health and SUD are few and far between. In recent years, addiction-focused centers of excellence have begun to emerge, often with a specific purpose or targeted intention. Some examples include: a focus on the barriers of rural addiction care, a mechanism to support insurance strategies for this patient population, or a governmental commitment for physician education.

Institutionally based centers of excellence would formalize the fact that addiction is a chronic condition. In the past few years, organizations have finally begun to recognize and embrace this concept for addiction care—the opioid crisis has made it impossible to ignore and increased the urgency to develop effective treatment. However, creating centers of excellence takes work and institutional prioritization.

> Institutionally based centers of excellence would formalize the fact that addiction is a chronic condition.

Gary De Carolis was determined to build his own small center of excellence to address the needs of patients who wanted to get healthy again. As the former executive director of the Turning Point Center of Chittenden County in Vermont, he took what began as an Alcoholics Anonymous clubhouse roughly fifteen years prior and grew it into the robust recovery support center it is now. He talks about the challenges of building this kind of resource, in terms of both serving those in recovery and obtaining the necessary funding to keep the lights on.

When I first started, we offered a safe space, but to be honest with you, even that was being compromised. When I first walked through the door, they were shooting up in the bathroom. They were passing drugs from one to another in the building. It was a shit show, to be honest with you, and anyone in good recovery would not come there to help support the recovery.

I witnessed more than one person who came very early in the recovery and within a week was back actively using in part because they met someone in the center. It really broke my heart. And so a big part of my early job was to change the culture of the center and make sure it was a safe place for people in recovery. If we could not give a good product to the community, then we were nothing.

We needed policies and procedures and not only on paper, but we had to actually do the hard work of implementing them. For example, those bathrooms that were being used for people to shoot up at times, we had to create a policy that says no more than one person could go in the bathroom at a time. And then one of our volunteers would go on in behind that person, check the bathroom and then come back out and lock it. And we locked the bathrooms too. We had to clamp down.

We had to change the furniture. When I first got there, there were three couches. Well, those are the worst things in the world for a recovery center. One, people fall asleep. Two, they can do things that you can't see. Over time, I changed the whole furniture structure to make it look more like a café, with tables and chairs where people could sit and talk to each other, play games … but not fall asleep on the couch.

And so with the help of a staff person or two that I hired, I'd say within two years, we made the necessary shift happen. You had people starting to see the center as a place. I had this wonderful woman named Meg Tipper walk through my door and say, "Would you be interested in having me do a yoga class here?" And I said, "Absolutely, let's do it." She started with one yoga class and we ended up having a recovery community yoga program there, probably six or seven yoga classes a week. Massage therapists would walk through the door. I had an instructor who was teaching people acupuncture, wanting to know if I'd be interested in having her students do internships in the center. I said, "Absolutely. Let's do that."

Gary noticed these changes were transforming how patients with SUD were seen and saw themselves. The organization shifted from a transitional place to a wellness center.

I realized quickly that not only was this helping someone go from actively using to being in recovery, but it was also taking a body that had been beaten to a pulp back to some degree of wellness. Over 50 percent of our guests were in their first year of recovery. And these things were all a part of helping create a wellness curriculum that would help their spiritual, physical, emotional, and mental selves.

This shift to wellness enabled Gary and his team to think bigger and more broadly about a patient's needs.

University of Vermont has the medical center here, and there's a program where you can write a proposal and a group of UVM medical students in their second year will come down and do some activity for the center. I knew the comorbidities were a big deal here. You have SUDs, but you also had BH disorders and other things. I could see that, but I didn't have anything tangible.

We came to agree upon doing a little study of comorbidity and it codified my thoughts—the three highest ones were anxiety, depression, and oral health. I went to some dentists and said, "Listen, oral health is a huge issue here for our guests. Would you be willing to come down and spend a morning doing an oral exam and then take it from there?" And sure enough, I was able to start that a couple of times a year and it made a huge difference.

The other thing that I started there was peer support specialists where there was always someone on the floor that, you walk through the door, and given that anxiety was a big issue for a lot of folks, someone was always on the floor who was in recovery themselves that would go over and ask, "How are you doing today? How is your recovery? And what can we do to support you?" You never felt like it was an unwelcoming environment. If anything, you felt just the opposite, it was very welcoming.

We got United Way funding three years ago. It'll end in June and then they can reapply, but that solidified everything. They gave me enough money. And the way this is worked out is there's a peer support specialist, a different one every day of the week. And I was able to have men and women, different drugs of choices, older, younger, ethnically, and racially diverse groups, so I could really create a place where everyone would feel welcome.

I always had the trust of my board behind me. They allowed me to do what I thought was necessary to help make the center a world-class organization. When I first started, we were renting our space and then there was a four-year capital campaign. The building itself that we're in now is so amazing. We were able to raise enough money to renovate the whole floor of a building we own now, so that it's made for recovery centers. It was purpose-built.

What's Needed

What Gary and other inspiring individuals like him have accomplished is remarkable. We need to not only replicate these initiatives but expand and codify them. To do this, we need to improve a variety of aspects of our care delivery system, as denoted below.

Cost of Care	Channels of Care	Multidisciplinary Approach	Roadmap
Track Total Cost of Care	Education	Empowering All Levels of Service	Consistent application of tools and skills to support care
Convert to Value-Based Care	Protocols	Coordinating Across Institutions and Departments	
	Accessible Guidelines		

Other countries have transformed their addiction care programs and have reaped substantial rewards. Iceland, for example, tackled SUD care delivery in recent years due to a rise in drug usage. They placed a special emphasis on the social aspects of treatment, such as ensuring there was a high availability of treatment and equity of access to care. In addition, both inpatient and outpatient services have been well integrated into a fluid addiction-treatment system, allowing for a comprehensive treatment model that recognizes SUD as a chronic disease. Given Iceland's small population size and its centralized healthcare system, it may have been easier for them to pivot and make progress. Nonetheless, they were able to make a sub-stantial impact and focused on the viable solutions.[44]

TREATMENT CENTERS

Treatment centers have been a long-standing and critical mechanism for patients to receive care. While barriers from affordability to visibil-ity to outcome measurements have been a limitation in this space, we also believe there is an opportunity to strengthen these programs. This field would benefit from increased business leadership, competition, and investment in this space. Given the prevalence of the disease and the impact on patients' lives, delivery of more affordable, quality-fo-cused, and patient-centered care within treatment centers is achieva-

---

44 Ingunn Hansdóttir, Valgerour Rúnarsdóttir, and Thorarinn Tyrfingsson, "Addiction Treatment in Iceland," *Textbook of Addiction Treatment: International Perspectives*, 2015.

ble. Engagement by experienced business leaders could transform the discipline and promote destigmatization at the same time. In this era of mission-focused businesses, we can see no greater cause.

This is the kind of model we need to develop in the US. Over the last few chapters, we've identified a number of strategies we can implement to pursue that agenda, such as the following:

➡ Reducing the cost of care

Any realistic approach must address the price tag. We can keep costs down by (1) using data to calculate a total cost of care, which will ultimately help us improve affordability, (2) transitioning from a volume-based care model to a value-based one, and (3) making effective holistic treatment accessible through medical provider offices.

➡ Improving the channels of care

By educating medical providers about long-term approaches to care, we immediately open doors to patients in need of holistic care, rather than episodic temporary fixes. We can also empower providers by giving them the tools they need to facilitate treatment, including protocols and accessible guidelines, thereby eliminating the burden of developing individualized treatment plans.

➡ Embracing a multidisciplinary approach

By establishing centers of excellence in the field of treatment, we create institutional focal points for the elevation of patient treatment. We also create another viable channel of care for patients.

EQUITY IN CARE

To build equitability, we must agree on the core values for each program and the critical few outcomes that will drive success. An important start is recognizing what should be the drivers of cost of care. At a minimum, we need to understand what factors should drive cost of care and what should not.

Factors That May Influence Cost of Care	Factors That Should Not Influence Cost of Care
Level of Care	Insurance Coverage
Length of Treatment	Operational Costs at Institution
Complexity of Patient's Co-Morbidities	Size of Staff at Institution
Complexity in Patient's Social Determinants	

We need to understand what factors should drive cost of care and what should not.

By doing all this, we create a foundation of care that is currently lacking in our system. With all that in place, our ultimate goal must be to develop a disruptive, innovative approach to treatment that slows or stops crises completely as well as prevents sequelae from developing. The best-case scenario is to prevent SUD from taking root in the first place. We'll discuss preventative strategies in the next chapter.

CHAPTER EIGHT

TREATMENT, PREVENTION, AND THE FUTURE OF CARE

You can't afford to get sick, and you can't depend on the present healthcare system to keep you well.

—ANDREW WEIL

Prevention of both the initial development of and subsequent progression of disease may be arguably some of the most important aspects of SUD care. We can have a significant impact on both minimizing substance-use exposures and—through active management of SUD—preventing disease progression. In this chapter, we'll dig into the approaches that hold the most promise in helping patients help themselves.

Going Beyond Our "Sick Care" System

As we hope we've made clear, America's approach to treatment is predominantly built around sick people seeking care. This is part of a larger trend in our healthcare system—most people only go for treatment when they have a specific ailment. While a short-term problem may be successfully remedied, the long-term health of the patient may not be addressed. Because providers are locked into a volume-based system, new patients enter the system as quickly as just-treated patients leave it, limiting a focus on wellness beyond the immediate and urgent need.

This system needs a reboot: we need to provide anticipatory care focused on *preventing* problems before they occur.

We're not wide-eyed idealists who believe addiction can be completely eliminated from the human condition. We know that's not a realistic target. But we can gain a fuller understanding of how to address SUD, combat it, and minimize its occurrence. While we recognize SUD is a very complex chronic disease, we have faith that we can have an impact.

This belief stems from the fact that we have, as a medical community, gone through this transformation before. Let's consider diabetes care. It took generations for diabetes mellitus treatment to evolve. For centuries, it was a death sentence for those who suffered from it. *Mellitus* is derived from the Latin word for *honey*, due to the sweetness of the urine. Ancient practitioners would see whether animals—for example, dogs or ants—were attracted to a patient's urine. In other words, if it were sweet like honey ... well, the patient had diabetes.

The main thing wrong with that system? That sweet taste means diabetes is already present—it's already too late to stop it from developing. An animal would only detect that sweetness if the patient were reliably peeing out glucose.

Similarly, today's SUD patients are generally only identified when it's too late. By that time, they are in the grips of an addiction that can be extremely difficult to address. Even though it's been roughly twenty years since addictions were finally acknowledged as chronic illnesses by the World Health Organization and the American Psychiatric Association, consistent protocols have yet to be created that approach those diseases *like* a chronic illness. It's not a stretch to say we're in our own dark ages in terms of dealing with SUDs. We may not be using animals to sniff out the sweetness of urine anymore (and thank goodness for that), but the level of sophistication of SUD prevention is still incredibly low and is often left to the school system's health class discussion rather than infused within medical care delivery.

Currently in diabetes care, we can identify those who are at risk of developing the disease and work with them on altering aspects of their lifestyles to prevent it from happening. This work is not easy, but diagnostic definitions of prediabetes are recognized. With SUDs, we generally wait for people to develop addictions, go in and out of crises, and possibly even exhibit sequelae before care is initiated. They end up coming to us, rather than our trying to mitigate issues before they develop. We fully recognize that diabetes and SUD are very different diseases; nonetheless, we submit there is value to considering where they may intersect.

Regardless, we hope you agree: for our care strategies to mature—for us to seriously combat the dangers of addiction

> We need to start focusing on *prevention.*

and put a dent in the economic and social costs of the illness—we need to start focusing on *prevention*.

A PATH TO PREVENTION

We all know how much damage a fire can cause to our residence. That's why we install smoke alarms. Obviously, if it goes off, you're warned there may be a fire and you now have the time to douse it before it grows too big to handle on your own. That allows you to avoid a lot of damage and expense to your home.

Applying this logic to SUD, the vast majority of SUDs have grown to the equivalent of an out-of-control blaze. Could we not save many lives and substantially lower healthcare costs by identifying the disease early on, giving us the possibility of providing effective early treatments? Could we not douse this metaphorical fire before it ravages someone's life?

We recognize that this smoke alarm analogy is a gross oversimplification of SUD. Part of this disease is a patient's inherent denial or difficulty with accepting the addiction and that it can take years for a patient or family to recognize just how detrimental the disease has become. But please bear with us for a moment—we submit that if stigma were eradicated, the chronic condition of SUD were normalized, and early intervention were emphasized, we could have a measurable impact on both the development of disease and disease progression.

When we consider prevention in SUD, we often think of abstinence from psychoactive or addictive drugs. This is only one of the types of prevention we should be considering. There are three different types of prevention we must focus on:

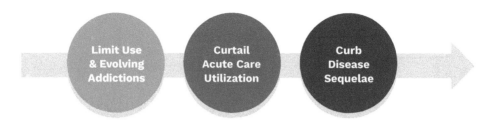

1. Limiting use and evolving addictions

In the best-case scenario, we would prevent people from developing SUDs in the first place. It is not realistic to imagine we could eradicate the disease entirely, but it's also irresponsible to just throw up our hands and say nothing more can be done. We must commit to developing proactive prevention strategies, based on data, that can help us in this effort. These can be targeted strategies to educate individuals about the risks associated with use; limit use in the clinical setting, such as the use of opioids for chronic pain; or intercept evolving addictions in those who are using drugs and/or prescribed medications. Further, monitoring patients along their journey can help flag warning signs of SUD before the disease fully takes hold.

2. Curtailing acute-care utilization

We must also be more proactive in preventing full-blown emergencies. The aftermath of these medical crises can be devastating. Patients who overdose can face a systemic shutdown of vital organs and poisoning from the acute toxicities of certain drugs. There are also the accompanying mental health crises that can evolve in this setting—including suicidality, depression, and anxiety and an exacerbation of psychotic episodes. Again, if we can create a robust coordinated care system that treats SUD as a chronic disease, we can potentially reduce our reliance on crisis care.

3. Curbing disease sequelae

Long-term SUD can result in a host of other related illnesses, such as endocarditis, liver failure, and cellulitis. All of which, obviously, will cause acute sickness that could lead to patients becoming infirm or even dying. Stopping serious SUD-related physical and mental challenges from occurring in the first place will go a long way toward helping us manage our patients' care. While this approach is not often viewed as disease *prevention*, we must recognize that preventing disease *progression* is perhaps equally important. These types of proactive interventions can provide substantial health benefits, lower the cost of care, and curb our reliance on crisis management. The longer a patient suffers from an active form of SUD, the more complex care grows, the costlier it becomes, and the more damaging it can be to the patient's long-term wellness.

EDUCATION, ENGAGEMENT, AND GAMIFICATION

A key mechanism to drive prevention is education for both patients and providers. There are a number of strategies that can optimize these educational efforts.

	Strategies to Optimize Patient Education	
1	Leverage Technology	Substantial advancements have been made in patient education beyond brochures and pamphlets to include mobile applications, gamification, and videos.
2	Accommodate Differences in Learning Styles	Different patients benefit from varying types of educational material. Ask them!
3	Recognize Language Barriers	Our patient populations are diverse. Language can be a substantial barrier for effective communication.
4	Consider Abilities and Accessibilities Such as Print-Size and Comfort with Technology	Differing educational, intellectual and physical capacities can create substantial barriers to educational efforts.
5	Empower Family Members and Loved Ones	Family members and loved ones often want to be engaged in care. They can reinforce the education along the process to recovery.
6	Support with Check-Ins	Patients will value care even that much further if you, as their provider, follow up and check in that educational resources are used and understood.

Education can benefit all chronic diseases, including SUD. According to a study in the *Journal of the American Osteopathic Association*, it only takes *forty-five minutes* of patient education to improve chronic disease outcomes.[45]

THE OTHER 45

Patients reported a greater understanding of their chronic disease and feeling better equipped to manage their health ... This is encouraging because these diseases typically require patients to take on a lot of responsibility in their care, often through changes in lifestyle.

—Alexis Stone, Lead Author, Other 45 Study

---

45 "Study Finds 45 Minutes of Patient Education Improves Chronic Disease Management," *Modern Health-care*, November 19, 2018, https://www.modernhealthcare.com/article/20181119/NEWS/181119936/study-finds-45-minutes-of-patient-education-improves-chronic-disease-management.

This study, known as the Other 45, took forty-seven patients suffering from chronic diseases such as hypertension, COPD, or diabetes and had them visit with a second-year medical student for forty-five minutes. That forty-five minutes turned out to be time well spent, as it measurably improved patients' attitudes and abilities in self-managing their care. Two more follow-up visits with the medical students were scheduled, one three weeks later and one three months later, and both times, the patients were assessed afterward through a forty-point questionnaire. The results after both follow-up sessions demonstrated consistent improvement in both the willingness and the ability to self-manage care. By giving these patients the knowledge and the tools they needed, they were empowered to take more control of their own wellness. That's a signal of significant progress because chronic illnesses require patients to take on a lot of responsibility for their own care, often through substantial changes in lifestyle.

This study was focused on an underserved community, where healthcare equity was lacking. Despite that, the patients responded well to their minischooling, gaining more confidence in navigating the healthcare system as well as upping self-care skills and techniques and self-monitoring. This boost in confidence had the effect of decreasing their emotional distress as well.

EDUCATING ON CHRONIC DISEASES

From an ethical perspective, it's also the right thing to do. As a nurse and a healthcare team member, I have to partner with the patient to understand what the chronic disease means to them, what their current situation is, and how we can best adapt our care plan to their needs so we drive the best outcomes for them as possible.

—Matthew Vitaska, Administrator of Outcomes, Effectiveness, and Patient Experience, Centura

Other research has buttressed these findings. For example, at Centura Health, a Colorado-based healthcare system, leaders made patient education a key component of their chronic-disease-management strategy and again measurably improved performance on certain outcomes.[46] However, Centura had a big challenge in implementing their patient education programs, as they ran nearly two hundred clinics across Colorado and Kansas. They needed a way to help them connect with and educate patients with chronic illnesses between office visits. They experienced limited success with mass emails, so they turned to tech for the solution.

They created interactive learning modules that could be used on mobile devices and computers to address preventive care and self-care management. Providers could send these modules to patients to help them self-educate. Matthew Vitaska, administrator of outcomes, effectiveness, and patient experience at Centura, described the goals of the modules thus: "Modules provide some didactic content but also have some videos in there and question and answer sessions to really engage the patient in their chronic condition to help drive optimal outcomes."[47] Vitaska found that it was most effective when

---

46   Sara Heath, "How Patient Education Tools Improve Chronic Disease Management," Patient Engagement Hit, January 9, 2017, https://patientengagementhit.com/news/how-patient-education-tools-improve-chronic-disease-management.

47   Ibid.

a clinician showed the patient how the modules worked during an in-person appointment, driving better patient engagement.

The interactive aspect of these types of mobile education tools is critical to their success. That's where *gamification* comes into play. The idea of gamification emerged from the computer science field and has been implemented in many other disciplines. Studies show having gamification inserted into educational modules can further improve engagement as well as a patient's ability to self-manage a chronic disease.[48]

Many web and mobile healthcare interventions currently do not inspire patients to use them at the level they should. Dry facts don't engage on their own; they simply don't appeal to many patients. Gamification of these educational modules facilitates engagement. It's not about turning them into actual games; it's about using game *elements*, including badges, levels, leader boards, and progress bars. The same types of engagement, reward, and incentive methodologies that game creators employ to keep players coming back are applied to encourage changes in behavior or motivate users to learn new skills. Even though the rewards are virtual in nature, they provide positive reinforcement. Medical apps such as SuperBetter and mySugr have used these types of gamification elements very successfully.

Gamification motivates patients with chronic illnesses to adhere to medication recommendations and self-manage their disease more effectively. It also supports adoption of digital healthcare services, as such adoption can be slow if the services are poorly designed or unwieldy to use. Considerations in deploying gamification strategies include the following:

---

48   Alaa AlMarshedi, Gary Wills, and Ashok Ranchhod, "Gamifying Self-Management of Chronic Illnesses: A Mixed-Methods Study," *JMIR Serious Games* 4, no. 2 (September 9, 2016).

Considerations for Effective Gamification

| Keep It Fun | Embed Progress, Feedback & Rewards | Consider Storytelling | Repetition is Key | Competition Can Be Motivating | Deploy Technology with User in Mind |

Singhal S, Hough J, Cripps D. 2019, "Twelve tips for incorporating gamification into medical education", MedEdPublish, 8, [3], 67, https://doi.org/10.15694/mep.2019.000216.1
van Gaalen, A.E.J., Brouwer, J., Schönrock-Adema, J. et al. Gamification of health professions education: a systematic review. Adv in Health Sci Educ (2020).
https://doi.org/10.1007/s10459-020-10000-3

We advocate the use of digital tools for both data collection and patient education. It's time for healthcare to improve the design of these tools and promote adoption. Everyone has a smartphone these days. Why not put these powerful devices to work to improve patient care?

Ideally, using technology, we could replicate the results of the study we referenced earlier, in which forty-seven patients were given forty-five-minute sessions with medical students to learn more about self-care

> We advocate the use of digital tools for both data collection and patient education.

of their chronic illnesses. Unfortunately, because our current healthcare system is under such financial pressure, most providers don't have the personnel or time to provide that kind of ongoing in-person education. That's why leveraging digital tools to take its place just makes sense. It's too expensive and time-consuming to deliver this information one-on-one to patients. However, with an effective digital delivery system, core educational concepts can be shared with each patient to better manage their own care between provider visits.

A colleague, Jamie Brandon, who has led educational programs at Aspenti Health, knows firsthand what happens when patients aren't given the tools needed to manage their pain medication.

My dad was about seventy-six years old and went in for a total knee replacement surgery. He went to a well-regarded hospital that did total joints and had all of the applicable accreditations, and had outpatient surgery.

Now in my role at Aspenti, one of the hats I wear is being the general manager of our e-learning business. We work to create educational content for other clinicians. And we were working on an "opioid stewardship" curriculum which would target providers. So I was interested in that data side. I asked my dad to show me what they gave him in terms of discharge paperwork around his pain meds.

So I took a look at all of this discharge stuff and it was a printed-out PowerPoint, and I flipped through it. And a lot of it was about wound dressings and how to care for the wound and the stitches. And then I got to pain management.

I think I still have a picture of it somewhere because I used it in a presentation once. It was one page, one printed slide and all it said was "Take your medication as prescribed." Well, my father was prescribed Oxycodone. And, underneath the Oxycodone, it had a line that just said "Narcan." And underneath that was a line that said something like, "You will be prescribed Advil, Tylenol, or other pain medication as required. Take the medicine as specified. Narcan may be also prescribed to be used if a loved one cannot wake you."

That's literally what it said and that's all it said. And I was like, "This is it? This is the whole rundown he's getting?"

So we go downstairs to the pharmacy in the hospital and he gets his prescription for Oxycodone. And I said, "Hey, we've got a script here for Naloxone or Narcan too." And they said, "Yeah, we have to prescribe it because it's a state law, but we don't actually always fill it. He's not going to need that." So he left without the Narcan, just the Oxycodone and went home.

He took the drug as prescribed, but less than twenty-four hours later, we were calling him and we noticed he sounded very lethargic and a bit tired. He was slurring his speech. He was at the point where he had to take a little ambulance ride back to the hospital because the Oxycodone was really affecting his system and had depressed his breathing.

I'm not a doctor, but my thesis is things affect him really strongly, and for whatever reason, the Oxycodone and the pain meds really messed with his system to the point where even now it's in his chart that they won't give him Oxycodone.

Was it scary? Yes. Was it tragic? No. Is it just completely silly and borderline irresponsible? Absolutely. We were evaluating the need for patient education for those prescribed opioids when I was literally in that experience.

If we're going to have medications like this and you're going to have protocols, then they need to be consistent, followed, and there have to be checks and balances in place. And there has to be a system that works. You can't send somebody home with a one-page sheet that says, "Use this if you can't wake them." Do better. Have a nurse come in and say, "Hey, here's Oxycodone. Here's what I want you to do."

Jamie's story isn't unusual, and it accents the need for effective patient education, which provides the following benefits:

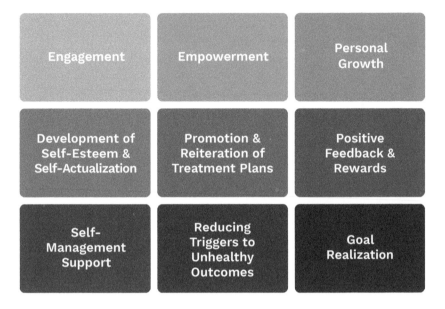

So why not focus on education if it provides these robust results?

Practical Applications of Digital Education

There are many ways digital modules can be applied. Suppose you have a loved one receiving MAT treatment for the first time. They might be stressed about the process, wondering what the experience will be like. Educational modules would walk them through MAT treatment and what's involved. Their family members, who might also be wondering what it's all about, could also use the module to learn more about what their loved one is going through.

You might wonder why patients couldn't just look up the information themselves on Google or another search engine. First of all, that particular form of research can be extremely unreliable—for example, people who use "Dr. Google" to self-diagnose get an accurate determination only one-third of the time, according to research published in the *Medical Journal of Australia*.[49] Second, when the patient's own provider offers course material, it simply has more impact. It elevates the discussion between provider and patient in a targeted way.

Here are three chronic diseases whose patients have benefitted from the introduction of digital tools.

➡ Obesity

Studies show that targeted weight-loss engagement technologies help patients not only reach weight-loss goals but also make permanent healthy lifestyle changes. In one case, a research team introduced a commercially available weight-loss tool to a group of sixty-eight middle-aged women who were identified as being overweight. Twenty-eight of them completed the twelve-month program. Those twenty-eight women lost an average of 16.5 pounds. They also saw an average 3.56" waist-circumference loss and lower blood pressure.[50]

➡ Diabetes

In the last thirty-four years, the diabetes population has grown by 314 million. Several digital tools have been developed to serve those who have diabetes—tools that make maintenance much easier. There are fewer needles involved and more real-time data available to ensure timely and precise responses to blood sugar levels.

For example, Abbott's FreeStyle Libre consists of a continuous glucose-monitoring unit with an insertable sensor and a small patch that is scanned using a reader or a smartphone app. The device can scan through layers of clothing, allowing for discretion and flexibil-

---

49   "New Research Finds 'Dr. Google' Is Almost Always Wrong," Medical Xpress, May 17, 2020, https://medicalxpress.com/news/2020-05-dr-google-wrong.html.

50   Sara Heath, "Digital Weight Loss Tools Improve Patient Engagement, Adherence," Patient Engagement Hit, January 12, 2017, https://patientengagementhit.com/news/digital-weight-loss-tools-improve-patient-engagement-adherence.

ity. It requires no finger-prick calibrations and gives precise enough data to dose insulin from it. In a study with 363 European type 2 diabetes patients, hemoglobin A1c results dropped by 1 percent due to use of the device, a significant decrease in the context of the small numbers being dealt with.

Another available tool is Sugar.IQ, a diabetes assistant app, much like Google's Siri or Amazon's Alexa. Sugar.IQ constantly tracks user information and compiles it in one place. It provides insights into how to most effectively keep glucose levels in the desired range. A study found that Sugar.IQ users spent 36 more minutes a day in range than they had before using the app. Episodes of low glucose levels also decreased by 0.95 a month and high glucose by 1.22.[51]

⇒ High blood pressure and cholesterol

The American Heart Association teamed up with Happify Health to create Happify Heart and Mind, a content platform designed to teach those with high blood pressure and high cholesterol how to reduce stress, increase the amount of heart-healthy foods in their diets, and engage in activities such as guided meditations, healthy meal-prep strategies, psychoeducational content, and goal-setting exercises. Happify Heart and Mind reduces the anxiety and depression that plague many with heart disease. Its effectiveness has been proven through several published studies. One randomized controlled trial found a 25 percent reduction in the symptoms of both anxiety and depression for those using Happify, when compared

---

51   Cara Dartnell-Steinberg, "Managing Diabetes: An Overview of Available Digital Tools," Mobi Health News, July 15, 2019, https://www.mobihealthnews.com/news/europe/managing-diabetes-overview-available-digital-tools.

with an active comparison condition—psychoeducation—used as directed by this study.[52]

We see no reason why SUD treatment can't enjoy similar success through the use of digital tools. Our organization's internal studies have shown that over 95 percent of patients have smartphone devices. The population is accessible; however, the gap lies in our ability to effectively engage our patients in and throughout recovery.

Providers may also find such tools beneficial. Many may not be up to speed on the latest best practices, especially primary care physicians who are responsible for the care of a wide range of medical conditions. Education modules can help grow their individual knowledge bases, inform their treatment, and hopefully provide a higher level of care as a result.

We developed what we call our Responsible Opioid Administration Solution (ROAS) for physicians and other caregivers. We offer certification in microcourses, which include foundational knowledge about opioid administration, core skills, competencies necessary to provide high-quality care, and decision-making guidelines on opioids and pain management, including how to discuss opioids with their patients and alternative pain medication that doesn't involve the use of opioids.

These are some SUD microcourse topics in an ever-evolving library:

- Evolution of the Opioid Crisis: From Pain Management to Overdose

---

52 "New Digital Tools Help People with High Blood Pressure and High Cholesterol make meaningful behavior change," American Heart Association, June 23, 2020, https://newsroom.heart.org/news/new-digital-tools-help-people-with-high-blood-pressure-and-high-cholesterol-make-meaningful-behavior-change.

- CDC Guideline for Prescribing Opioids for Chronic Pain

- Administering Naloxone

- Urine Drug Testing: Effective Use and Scenarios

- Approaching a Patient Suspected of Misusing Opioids

- Educating Patients on Safe Opioid Storage and Disposal

- Techniques for Compassionate Tapering

Some behavioral health microcourse topics in an ever-changing library include these:

- The Toll of Outbreaks and Natural Disasters on the Healthcare System and Healthcare Workers

- First, Heal Thyself: Recognizing Early Warning Signs of Mental Health Distress

- Back to Basics: Self-Care for Healthcare Professionals

- Resilience Training: Building Skills to Thrive

- Managing Energy Using Mindfulness, Meditation, and Breathwork

We've discussed the importance of developing a holistic approach to care by thinking more broadly and deeply about the mechanics of treatment. But, in a truly holistic care model, treatment is your plan B. Prevention should be the priority, both for the patient's well-being and our healthcare system's solvency. We want to avoid expensive and harmful emergencies as well as life-threatening sequelae. Most of all, we want to prevent SUD from developing in the first place.

The decision to prioritize prevention over treatment, however, is one that has to be made at *every* touchpoint of care—from regulators and policy makers to hospital executives, care teams, thought leaders, and passionate change agents across the country.

In the next chapter, we'll look at the roles of these stakeholders in the chain of care and reveal the four pillars of what we believe is the foundation of any holistic approach to patient care.

CHAPTER NINE

REACHING THE SUMMIT: A REDESIGNED BEHAVIORAL HEALTHCARE MODEL

An individual can make a difference, but a team can make a miracle.

—DOUG PEDERSON

Our collective failure to adequately address SUD in our country has cost us dearly, both economically and socially. Addiction has continued to skyrocket throughout (and possibly because of) the pandemic—but is still largely being ignored because COVID has been such an overwhelming health challenge for providers to get their arms around. Yes, it will be a great day when COVID has finally been tamed (which will hopefully be by the time you read this book). The downside, however, is that we'll be left with an even bigger SUD problem than we began with. The stakes for revamping our treatment approach could not be higher.

We've already discussed some broad, innovative, and disruptive strategies for implementing meaningful change that will expand access to treatment, create robust prevention methodologies, and empower us to respond to the realities of SUD care. However, discussion is simply not enough. We need to go beyond words and make a collective commitment to putting those strategies into action.

In this chapter, now is the time to really dig in to understand how to practically implement these strategies.

A Pyramid of Progress

At the core of any effort in healthcare stands its triple aim: lower costs, higher quality of care, and increased access. To achieve true equity and complete our mission, these three goals must be reached.

The pyramid of progress represents what we believe needs to be done to improve SUD treatment.

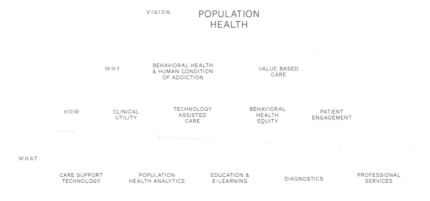

Pyramid of Progress

As with Maslow's hierarchy of needs, *vision* is a central component here: we must embrace a population health management approach. While the definitions of population health management vary slightly, the basic idea is to improve the quality of care and outcomes for a defined group of people. By utilizing data and tracking results of a specific population, we can ultimately determine what works and what doesn't for individual patients. This approach will aid in the evolution of not only SUD care but also basic medical care for all.

So what's in the way of making progress?

For that answer, we need only to look at the second tier of our pyramid, which represents the *why* of things being what they are. That *why* can be directly traced to how SUD issues collide with our current system, in which SUD is not managed as a chronic condition that requires ongoing care.

From there, we move down to the third tier of our pyramid, representing *how* to create the change we all want to see. In that tier, you'll see there are four areas of opportunity that we believe will bring us closer to the objectives we seek. They are as follows:

1. Clinical utility

This is our mantra—*if it doesn't help clinically, it isn't worth doing.* This vision of clinical care is broad, one that centers on the health and well-being of our patients. *Utility* refers to care that has been proven to be beneficial through an evidence-based, outcome-based approach. If we focus on actions that have shown efficacy, we can generate more positive treatment results.

This is our mantra— if it doesn't help clinically, it isn't worth doing.

2. Technology-assisted care

We providers are doing the best possible job we can within a difficult system. We fill our days trying to respond to patients in a timely manner by keeping up with events in their lives that might impact treatment and supporting whatever progress they've managed to make. In addition, we unfortunately also commit a substantial amount of time to the myriad administrative burdens that come with the job.

Bottom line? *We* need support. Automation and technological tools must be leveraged. These approaches represent a cost-effective solution that can free us up to care for our patients and allow for human connection.

Technology-assisted care programs should be designed to facilitate clinical workflows. When properly designed, they can also lead us to the best treatment approaches as well as those with the highest clinical utility. Healthcare is in its infancy in truly embracing management platforms that can assist in promoting best practices, empower patients, and leverage current technological resources to drive care. With an overstretched workforce, TAC can become an asset to track patients, comply with regulatory standards, automate documentation, and promote standards. TAC that promotes population health management should reach beyond the typical functionality of an electronic health record. TAC tools can facilitate core clinical operations.

3. Behavioral health equity

We need care that is *equitable*. Morally, healthcare must be equitable, fair, and available to all our citizens, or we are failing them and their loved ones. In addition, there are sound financial reasons to pursue health equity. Underserved populations can require care delivery that takes the form of expensive acute services. This approach can increase the cost of care and lead to severe health risks. A value-based care model focused on this patient population would not only achieve behavioral health equity but also result in less costly and more effective care.

4. Patient engagement

For any chronic disease, patient engagement is a critical element to success. This is particularly essential for SUD patients. Virtually every action that supports patient engagement can improve outcomes. When the provider takes time to establish a trusting and open relationship, the patient is more likely to adhere to regimens and stay committed to recovery. This is where the behavioral therapy of contingency management could make an important difference. Contingency management uses motivational incentives and tangible rewards to help a person refrain from drugs and/or alcohol use. To encourage sobriety and healthy behavior options, patients receive rewards when they obtain positive goals and make lifestyle changes within their day-to-day lives. These rewards can be based on such criteria as drug-free urine specimens or consistent treatment attendance.

Finally, the bottom tier of our pyramid represents the *what*, the tools need to leverage the areas of opportunity. These include care-support technology, population health analytics, education and e-learning, and diagnostics and professional services. Patients deserve the best care possible and all tools at our disposal need to be deployed. Care support technology optimizes patient engagement and outcomes as well as simplifies and standardizes clinical operations. Population health analytics provide the tracking mechanism not only to validate the technological advancements but also to offer much-needed insight into patients' risks and pain points. Education and e-learning enable the tools to disseminate the new-found knowledge and to ensure that everyone—from patients to providers to community health partners—is armed with the best information to drive success. Finally, professional services and diagnostics provide additional insights and support for an overtaxed system.

A Road Map to Success

Even the best treatment providers and organizations can improve and enhance our delivery of care. We applaud those engaged in an assess-and-improve mindset. This section will provide a practical, hands-on approach to achieve holistic success in SUD care.

Our organization has provided consultation to other healthcare organizations, aiding in their progress toward their goals to develop SUD programs and achieve excellence. We have provided proactive organizational-performance-management support to develop an understanding of baseline performance and identify key areas for improvement. We hope to arm you with some of these tools so that you can perform your own discovery, implement change, and reap the rewards of these efforts.

Let's explore the three stages central to any successful project:

Assessment	Implementation	Achievement

A breakdown of the steps of each phase is provided in the following graphic. We will walk through each of these.

Stages

Assessment			Implementation			Achievement		
Phases	Deliverables	Tools	Phases	Deliverables	Tools	Phases	Deliverables	Tools
Discovery	• Engage assessment team • Stakeholder interviews/surveys	• Review healthcare ecosystem map • Institutional Assessment Index tool (IAI) • Self-assessment tool	Design	• Kick-off • Workflow analysis and design • Interface and conversion specifications • Training plans • Resource plan	• Implementation project plan template	Measure	• Monthly fee / profit and loss • Variable management	• Enterprise analytics platform and financial planning resources
Base Line	• Calculate IAI score • Refine gaps and opportunities • Determine clinical outcomes • Determine financial outcomes	• Achievement index score card • Assessment survey summary • Gap analysis template	Build	• EHR interfacing • Navigator installation • IQ enterprise knowledge platform • Client Achieve 360 insights and dashboards • Application build and system set • Data mapping • Validation • Training	• Implementation project plan template • kick-off meeting template	Monitor	• Contract management and performance management	• Enterprise analytics platform and financial planning resources
Identify	• Project charter • Expectation alignment presentation • Defining scope • Resource allocation • Pricing • Targets assignment • Contracting, if applicable	• Program charter template	Activate	• Activation audit • Simulation and LIVE planning • Live time frame and management • Navigator recovery support assignments and tracking • Transition to service	• Quarterly review template	Evaluate	• Baseline / post implementation comparison • Risk / reward management	• Quarterly review template

ASSESSMENT

The Assessment stage has three phases, which are discovery, establishing a baseline, and identifying a project. Given the criticality of this phase, we have outlined some important deliverables and armed you with a number of tools.

Assessment		
Phases	Deliverables	Tools
Discover	• Engage assessment team • Stakeholder interviews / surveys	• Review healthcare ecosystem map • Institutional achievement index tool (IAI) • Self-assessment tool
Baseline	• Calculate IAI score • Refine gaps and opportunities • Determine clinical outcomes • Determine financial outcomes • Identify mechanisms to achieve goals	• Achievement index score card • Assessment survey summary • Gap analysis template
Identify	• Project charter • Expectation alignment presentation • Defining scope • Resource allocation • Pricing • Targets assignment • Contracting, if applicable	• Program charter template

Discovery

During the discovery phase, it is important to engage a diverse team of stakeholders. You may want to review the healthcare ecosystem map (chapter 3) to consider the breadth of care delivery provided to the SUD population. Further, the organization's Institutional Achievement Index (chapter 6 and below) can be a useful reference point.

SUD Institutional Achievement Index

Core Competencies	Level 1	Level 2	Level 3	Level 4	Level 5	Level 6
Collaborative stewardship	Minimal or no collaboration or leadership in a fee-for-service health payment model	Establishment of leadership with nascent collaboration in a fee-for-service health payment model	Engaged collaboration and leadership support in a fee-for-service payment model without effective mechanisms to monitor impact and progress	Leadership and collaboration with the implementation of programmatic performance indicators and consideration of a value-based care payment model	Engaged leadership and/or governance monitoring collaborative impact with transitioning to value-based care payment system	Ongoing, monitored progress demonstrating effective leadership and collaboration within a value-based care payment system
Evidence-based care	Holistic management of Substance Use patients, including social aspects of health, is not achieved. Little to no standard protocols or identification of potential care gaps exist.	Care delivery is focused on the current episode of care with increased recognition of the importance of downstream clinical outcomes. Initial commitment of resources with little to no standard protocols or visibility to potential care gaps	Care delivery has an increased focus on employment of best practice standards with identification of disease sequelae and comorbidities in addition to the active management of patient. Resources are being developed for standard protocols to emerging care gaps	Care delivery supports best practices with the identification of disease sequelae and co-morbidities. Committed resources and standard protocols are in development. Care gaps are recognized but only addressed in a limited way	The organization has developed a holistic care model with adoption of best practices and emerging mechanisms to identify comorbidities and disease sequelae. There is a commitment of adequate resources, standard protocols and recognition of care gaps	There is an organization wide commitment to best practice standards and mechanisms to identify disease co-morbidities and sequelae. Fully integrated resources and standard protocols are available and integrated across all care transitions
Chronic care management	No significant adoption of chronic care management model	Early recognition of SUD as a chronic disease model with an appreciate of care continuum	Recognition of chronic care model with developing standard resources focused on Substance Use Disorders	Adoption of chronic care model with developing standardized resources across care continuum including prevention, pain management and Substance Use Disorders	Adoption of chronic care model with increasing standardization and focus on prevention and early diagnosis efforts	System-wide adoption of chronic disease model with prioritization on prevention and established standards of care
Patient engagement	Minimal patient/family engagement outside of traditional care models	Initial development of mechanisms to engage patients/families	Patient engagement strategies are being deployed with an active development of processes to improve patient care or experience. Families are not directly engaged outside of traditional clinical care model	Patient engagement strategies are actively deployed with an evolving consideration of the patient's family and/or community involvement in the patient's care	Patients are actively engaged in their own care with increasing involvement of family and/or community	Patients, families and/or community are actively engaged in care with patients driving continued improvements in care for themselves and others

At the heart of the SUD Institutional Achievement Index are four core competencies that any organization managing SUD should consider paramount to success. These are collaborative stewardship, evidence-based care, chronic care management, and patient engagement, as described below.

We have provided a self-assessment tool at the end of the book that crosswalks to the SUD Institutional Achievement Index. This self-assessment tool can be used to determine where your organization stands on each of these core competencies. Use this self-assessment to identify gaps and opportunities for quality-improvement projects and embrace a more holistic, population-health-based model for addiction care. Each of the competencies has underlying measures that help an organization not only determine where they stand but also shine light on what can be done to have highly successful SUD care delivery. Each competency receives a score based on the following bullets from one to five that can be crosswalked to identified levels. The average of each of these core competencies determines one's overall level in the maturity model.

Since they are crucial to the delivery of high-quality care in SUD, we will provide an overview of these four core competencies:

Collaborative stewardship—management of SUD requires organization-wide leadership and collaborative participation, engaging both internal and external community resources. Stewardship, including management of financial resources, is imperative. Critical components include the following:

- Leadership and/or governance

- Care coordination

- Communication

- Monitoring

- Payment models

Evidence-based care—peer-reviewed literature demonstrates that MAT works. Adoption of best-practice standards is essential for the holistic management of patients with or at-risk for SUD. Continued tracking of patient outcomes optimizes care and allows for program enhancements and adaptations. These are some critical components:

- Capacity

- Training

- Protocols

- Care gaps / transitions of care

- SAoH

Chronic care management—SUD is a chronic disease that needs to be managed along the entire care continuum. Care delivery needs to include prevention, management of at-risk populations, disease treatment, and addressing of disease sequelae. Critical components include these:

- Recognition of chronic disease

- Prevention

- Population health approach

- Centers of excellence

- Harm reduction

Patient engagement—Patient and family engagement is essential for the patient's journey to recovery. Organizations must adopt practices that enhance patient, family, and community engagement and optimize the patient experience. Critical components include the following:

- Strategies of empowerment

- Patient advisors/ambassadors

- Tracking progress

- Soliciting feedback

- Technology

Baseline

Establishing a baseline from which to improve is an essential part of any program development. As outlined by the CDC, establishing a baseline can help in these ways:

- Serve as a reference point

- Allow for demonstrable change

- Monitor ongoing progress

- Flag particular areas for opportunities

After capturing a baseline, socialize the findings throughout the organization so that everyone is metaphorically and literally on the same page. We have provided some tools that will facilitate the efforts to socialize the baseline findings.

For example, the results of the SUD Institutional Achievement Index can be used to form an Achievement Index Scorecard or Summary Report (see graphic below). These summative reports can serve as a valuable metric of where the organization started on its journey for program improvement.

Sample Summary Report

Collaborative Stewardship

LEVEL 3

Adoption of a value-based care model

Incorporation of behavioral health, medical and community...

Monitor progress with institutional dashboards &...

Collaborative and unified provider engagement

Effective leadership and/or governance

Adoption of SU management as an organization wide priority

Evidence-Based Care

LEVEL 4

Social aspects of health are incorporated into practice...

Co-morbidities and disease sequelae are anticipated and...

Addresses unique needs of rural communities

Ready access to integrated SU and Pain management...

Providers feel confident in SU management

Implement workflow & care teams to manage care...

Standardize clinical strategies to minimize variation in care

Sufficient capacity for managing SU patients

Sample Scorecard Report
Used to objectively analyze for IAI model

Core Competencies & Imperatives	Levels					
	1	2	3	4	5	6
Collaborative Stewardship			X			
Leadership & Governance				X		
Care Coordination					X	
Communication	X					
Monitoring		X				
Payment Models		X				
Evidence-Based Care				X		
Capacity						X
Training					X	
Protocols		X				
Care Gaps & Transitions of Care			X			
Social Determinants of Health			X			
Chronic Care Management				X		
Recognition of SUD as a Chronic Disease				X		
Prevention			X			
Population Health Approach			X			
Centers of Excellence				X		
Harm Reduction				X		
Patient Engagement				X		
Strategies of Empowerment			X			
Patient & Family Advisors or Ambassadors		X				
Tracking Progress					X	
Soliciting Feedback			X			
Technology	X					

Depending upon the organization's needs and predilections, a more descriptive format can be used:

Assessment Survey Summary

Organization: _____

Substance Use Management Assessment

Institutional Achievement Index
Summary & Findings: Level 3

The organization has achieved an Institutional Achievement Index score that demonstrates overall good performance in the programmatic approach to SUD/BH care. While some noted gaps are identified, the organization has made substantial progress to date.

Core Competencies:
Collaborative Stewardship: Level 3

Engaged collaboration and leadership support in a fee-for-service health payment model without effective mechanisms to monitor impact and progress

- Effective leadership and/or governance is driving collaboration
- Providers communicate routinely regarding specific patients
- Periodic collaborative meetings to understand one another's workflow and expertise; however, formal care teams are not developed
- Performance indicators and/or dashboards have been discussed but not implemented
- Fee-for-service health payment models predominate

Evidence-Based Care:
Level 4

Care delivery supports best practices with the identification of disease sequelae and co-morbidities. Committed resources and standard protocols are in development. Care gaps are recognized but only addressed in a limited way.

- Buprenorphine waivered providers with understanding of capacity and demand for SU patients
- Providers are capable of managing SU patients and receive some community support
- Easily accessed and integrated SU and Pain management resources with limited use
- Evolving recognition of potential care gaps/care transitions
- Patients are managed holistically with anticipation of and identification of co-morbidities and disease sequelae
- Social aspects of health are not yet incorporated into practice management

Chronic Care Management
Level 4

Adoption of chronic care model with developing standardized resources across care continuum including prevention, pain management and Substance Use Disorders

- Chronic care model is accepted with some influence on care
- Leadership is emphasizing need for prevention and early diagnostic services
- Early risk stratification is recognized as a critical component of care but minimal adoption
- Integration of services across pain, SUD and SUD sequelae with several shared resources is seen
- Harm reduction strategies are commonly used

Patient Engagement
Level 3

Patient engagement strategies are being deployed with an active development of processes to improve patient care or experience. Families are not directly engaged outside of traditional clinical care model

- Strategies and specific mechanisms to empower and engage patients and families are being actively developed
- Patient advisory groups or patient ambassadors are being recruited for involvement in care settings
- Patient access to clinical information is extended to web-based portals and with some targeted literature/ educational content
- Community-based lecture series have been introduced to engage interested community members in care topics
- Patients are beginning to see themselves as champions of their own care
- Little discrete resources or time has been allotted to engage family and/or loved ones in patient's care

205

Once your findings have been summated, they can be shared across your organization. We have added one additional tool to drive home to your colleagues the criticality of the work that remains. The Gap Analysis Template tool, which can be found at the end of the book, enables you to input identified gaps from the assessment and map out next steps. These steps include defining scope, aligning expectations, allocating resources, assigning targets, and pricing or contracting, as applicable. We hope that providing these templates and examples facilitates conversation within your organization.

Identify

In the words of Desmond Tutu, "There is only one way to eat an elephant: a bite at a time." While centers of excellence are an important long-term consideration nationally, not all of us can commit to a programmatic approach in one step.

If the appetite or resources are not available for a broad-based initiative, you still can make small, incremental improvements that will have a real impact for patients and their families. We have provided a Program Charter Template at the end of this book to kickstart your efforts.

IMPLEMENTATION

Implementation		
Phases	**Deliverables**	**Tools**
Design	• Kick-off • Workflow analysis and design • Interface and conversion specifications • Training plans • Resource plan	• Implementation project plan template
Build	Possible considerations: • EHR interfacing • Access to educational resources • Access to analytics and dashboards • Application build and system set • Data mapping • Validation • Process mapping • Training	• Implementation project plan template • Kick-off meeting template
Activate	• Activation audit • Simulation and LIVE planning • Live timeframe and management • Assignments and tracking • Transition to service	• Quarterly review template

Like the Assessment stage, Implementation has three phases as well: design, build, and activate. Since the path for implementation depends on the project itself, we cannot be as prescriptive in this section. However, we will introduce some basic principles of change management that should help you on your way.

In the words of George Bernard Shaw, "Progress is impossible without change." To paraphrase Charles Darwin, those who demonstrate adaptability to their environment survive and thrive. The ever-evolving healthcare landscape—with monumental shifts in the fields of behavioral health and addiction medicine—requires progress and an ability to improve our care delivery. Getting organization buy-in and colleague engagement can, at times, feel like a Sisyphean task. We will walk you through some foundational steps to support these critical initiatives.

Design

Any project, regardless of how big or small, should begin with a plan. A well-considered implementation plan allows the team to get behind the idea and provide a path forward. It helps socialize the idea and the requirements and keeps the project focused and tracking to agreed-upon timelines. A sample Project Implementation Plan Template has been provided at the back of the book for your reference. Specific attention to personnel training and competency, financial and operational resources, and the impact on your team's workflow and performance is crucial.

Build

According to Guy Kawasaki, "Organizations are successful because of good business implementation, not good business plans." This is where the rubber meets the road. While it is important to be organized and think ahead, nothing trumps a solid implementation.

The milestone of beginning must be acknowledged. Meet with colleagues for the kickoff, focusing on motivating the work and inspiring engagements. A Kickoff Meeting Template has been provided at the back of this book to facilitate this important step. A substantial amount of time should be allotted for discussion during this first meeting. While it is important that the project be organized and orchestrated, it is a key time to promote the objectives of this project. This may be when our colleagues are most enthusiastic and excited for change, so make sure you use the time wisely. You may also encounter those who may be resistant to change. Try to identify these individuals *in advance* of the meeting to allow them a chance to process the change and buy-in to the need for change. Not surprisingly, it overlaps some with the Project Implementation Plan

Template, as the kickoff meeting is a mechanism for launching the Implementation Plan.

Consistency and laser focus are essential at this point in the program. There will be inevitable desire to scope creep and extend resources toward adjacent efforts, but discipline and constancy will allow the project to succeed. Consider frequent check-ins offline with key stakeholders to support their work and motivate the team.

Activate

If you are reaching this final phase, you are almost there! If it hasn't already, this is where project fatigue—the loss of focus that can come from a lot of tasks over a long period of time—often kicks in. You may even find that team members see the project as complete, the tasks accomplished, and are ready to move on. Don't give in now! You are ready to go! The project has been underway, and the team is prepared to launch.

Set up a prelaunch party to tie off lose ends and to celebrate the work to date. Invite a broad cross section of interested parties and/or socialize through emails, social media, or other appropriate outlets. Whenever possible, consider a soft launch, a pilot, or a beta with a subsection of individuals or teams. These smaller units allow for quick adjustments that inevitably follow any implementation process. This is a time to stay positive and celebrate the effort. There may be unexpected obstacles in the activation process, but remember these are small relative to the overall scope of the project. Don't forget to summarize where the project has landed: identify whether you hit preestablished targets like budget and timeframes; recap on the success metrics and how they were met; and address new ideas that have been inspired by the project. We have provided a Quarterly Project Review Template that, while generally advisable for the

Achievement phase, can provide a mechanism to help to socialize early wins.

ACHIEVEMENT

Achievement		
Phases	Deliverables	Tools
Measure	• Monthly fee / profit and loss • Variable management	• Enterprise analytics platform and financial planning resources
Monitor	• Contract management and performance management	• Enterprise analytics platform and financial planning resources
Evaluate	• Baseline / post-implementation comparison • Risk / reward management	• Quarterly review template

This stage is where you reap the rewards of all that time and effort. This is how you show success and ensure this work is sustainable and not passed by.

Like the other stages, Achievement has three phases: measure, monitor, and evaluate. If grant funded, most sponsors insist on completing at least the measure phase. Most will want to see a mechanism to monitor. Most organizations will want the same thing to show a return on investment. We've inserted the third phase, evaluate, to recognize that for a truly implemented plan, we need to consistently be reviewing our data and making improvements. The evaluate phase provides a feedback loop for future quality-improvement projects and continuous growth.

Measure

Prior to initiating this project, there were key performance metrics that had organizational buy-in and commitment. Now is the time to demonstrate the gains from this effort. This can be done through leveraging off-the-shelf data analytical tools or utilizing current existing data software strategies. Consider all stakeholders when evaluating performance, noting operational, quality, financial, satisfaction, and regulatory needs.

Monitor

Ongoing monitoring ensures these critical projects don't lose their traction and impact. Monitoring can foster a growth and quality-improvement culture. Quarterly reviews and/or analytical dashboards can give broad visibility to the success of the implementation project and help stakeholders see the importance of the work. A sample Quarterly Project Review Template is provided at the end of this book.

Evaluate

While periodic monitoring tracks progress and change, occasional reflective evaluation of these metrics is also an important strategy. Evaluation allows organizations to see the overall impact by comparing preimplementation baseline data to current data. This can be an important celebration of hard work and improve the overall self-efficacy of the organization.

A Team Effort

Whatever your healthcare role is, you can play an important part in creating the change that is necessary and overdue. You undoubtedly have faced frustrations with the system as currently structured. Our hope is this book offers some light at the end of the tunnel for fixing the most egregious deficits in our healthcare delivery for this patient pool.

With that in mind, we'd like to identify what we believe to be the most important stakeholders in this effort, what their current struggles are, and how they can help turn the tide.

Let's look at these groups in turn.

HEALTHCARE EXECUTIVES

Who They Are:

Hospital CEOs, inpatient/outpatient addiction center leadership, and other individuals in positions of authority in the healthcare system. These folks may be the deciders because a word from them can often move mountains. These leaders often represent the largest employers in their respective communities, so they can wield substantial power in the process.

Some Challenges:

A challenge might be to drastically improve the quality of care in the face of cost-based pressures. Because a volume-based system prevails, it can be difficult for positive disruption to take place. Any effort can be expensive and time-consuming although mighty rewards can be reaped.

How They Can Help:

Because they are in positions of authority, healthcare executives can lead the charge in promoting and implementing much-needed change that will help put SUD patients on the road to recovery.

CARE TEAMS AND THOUGHT LEADERS

Who They Are:

MAT care teams, including nurses, physicians, counselors, office staff, behavioral therapists, recovery coaches, and peer-support counselors. This group is often composed of committed caregivers who most likely have experience providing SUD treatment. Some may even be in recovery themselves.

Some Challenges:

A lack of funding poses a critical challenge, limiting holistic care and programmatic offerings and driving burnout. These professionals have become frustrated and tired of the lack of progress in creating effective care protocols. Every day, they are faced with inconsistent standards and methods to engage patients in a more complete and coordinated care system.

How They Can Help:

Give visibility to obstacles and work to adopt programmatic strategies using data that can be shared and disseminated to payers for better support. Because they are at the ground level in our fight to provide better strategies, they can provide invaluable input to enhance those strategies from a realistic viewpoint.

REGULATORS, POLITICIANS, AND POLICYMAKERS

Who They Are:

These are individuals who impact policy at both the federal and state levels. State lawmakers understand the local political climate and what will work with the existing healthcare structure. We've seen a variety of infrastructure strategies engineered at the state level.

Some Challenges:

Obstacles can include balancing the need to support families and the communities while determining how to leverage available funds to drive projects.

How They Can Help:

Work with communities to understand existing gaps in care and set up task forces to drive change. They can also prioritize aid to prevention and treatment.

PASSIONATE CHANGE AGENTS

Who They Are:

Community members who've been touched by the SUD crisis and have made the decision to step up and help—perhaps by volunteering at a treatment center, acting as a recovery coach, serving as an advocate, or spearheading grassroots support programs like needle exchanges. This group can include members of the police force, local politicians, care providers, and motivated members of the general public.

Some Challenges:

This group has several challenges, including these:

1. The fragmentation of care makes it difficult to see the challenge holistically.

2. There is no avenue for empowerment. To really create change, this group requires the ways and means to effectively champion the cause.

3. They lack funding. These kinds of change agents often work at the grassroots level through community efforts that are conducted on shoestring budgets.

How They Can Help:

Team up with larger foundations and organizations that can supply the needed resources. Drive data by insisting treatment programs have metrics and focus on critical outcomes. Above all, bring more visibility to this crisis.

Stakeholders can make an incredible difference by bringing together coalitions and resources to expand care to those who need it desperately.

* * *

This chapter poses a big ask—to fundamentally change treatment strategies. Nonetheless, this kind of meaningful evolution is necessary. What we're doing now just isn't working—not for the patients, the providers, or our underserved communities.

But to fight and eventually truly impact SUD, we're going to need decision-makers to step up, both in healthcare and in policy development. Stakeholders, including care teams and passionate change agents, are critical to this effort. Everyone must lift together. From the grassroots level all the way up to our most powerful political leaders in Washington, DC, there will need to be a top-to-bottom alignment in our objectives and the methodologies designed to help us reach patients.

The stakes are high, and the obstacles loom large. But by uniting around a wellness-oriented road map to care, we can turn the tide of this brutal epidemic. We can promote transformation in the lives of our patients. We can prevent SUD from developing in the first place. We can drastically reduce the number of ED-centered, high-risk, high-cost crisis-care episodes. And we can stop sequelae in their tracks—keeping individuals, families, and communities solvent, happy, and healthy.

> But to fight and eventually truly impact SUD, we're going to need decision-makers to step up, both in healthcare and in policy development.

We are putting all our energies into that endeavor—and we hope you will too.

What gives me hope really is always just, you never know when someone is going to turn that corner. When someone is going to make staying clean the most important thing in their life and they are going to go about saving their own life. And we see it happen and it happens regularly and it's really important to keep an eye on that and how people do well and people can change. I have seen people who I would have bet you a jillion dollars would never get clean, get clean. And I always bear that in mind. You just never know. Miracles happen. They happen all the time.

—Brooky Sherwood,
Registered Nurse and Addiction Specialist

THE WAY FORWARD

*If you're walking down the right path and you're willing
to keep walking, eventually you'll make progress.*

—BARACK OBAMA

"Purdue Pharma LP will plead guilty to three felonies and pay $8.3 billion to settle federal probes of how it marketed OxyContin, the highly addictive painkiller blamed for helping spark the US opioid epidemic."[53]

We're pleased that action is finally being taken against those who have irresponsibly spurred our current SUD crisis. However, we can't let this type of recompense distract us from the fact that there are still too many afflicted with this chronic disease and that the numbers are growing every day. The COVID-19 pandemic has only made matters worse. Although the complete data wasn't available for 2020 at the time of this writing, a health alert published by the CDC at the end of the year reported a "concerning acceleration" in overdose deaths

---

53   Jef Feeley and Chris Strohm, "Purdue Pharma to Plead Guilty, Pay $8.3 Billion Over Opioids," Bloomberg, October 21, 2020, https://www.bloomberg.com/news/articles/2020-10-21/purdue-pharma-said-to-pay-8-billion-to-settle-opioid-probes.

for 2020, which provisional data shows is on track to be *the deadliest year for US drug overdose deaths in recorded history*.[54] Lockdowns and social distancing have only made those who suffer from SUD more likely to relapse in order to cope with the anxiety and depression caused by the virus.

SUD represents the greatest ongoing healthcare crisis of our time. It's claiming more lives than cancer. Despite throwing billions of dollars at the problem, government agencies, healthcare institutions, and grassroots programs are not making the kind of progress that's necessary to truly create the new paradigm of care to reverse this deadly tide. Right now, an overwhelming majority of recovered patients eventually relapse.

We must unite around a universal road map to recovery—a philosophy of care that prevents addiction, emergencies, and sequelae, helping those who *are* addicted maintain a lifelong recovery. At the most essential level, this strategy is going to need to acknowledge and respond to the reality that addiction is a chronic illness—one that is predictable and manageable but, as far as we know, incurable.

Given that addiction is a lifelong illness, our strategy must reflect our patients' broader health profiles as well as the realities of their lives, including SAoH. We must use data to develop tactical treatment plans, support bedside care tools, and calculate the total cost of care. These kinds of measures will ultimately help us develop a value-driven approach to care: one that is equitable for patients from all walks of life. That approach must be affordable, accessible, and powered by centers of excellence.

Ultimately, the more we learn from data we collect, the more we can *educate*. We can properly teach and train patients, providers

---

54   Zachary Siegel, "The Deadliest Year in the History of US Drug Use," *New York*, December 23, 2020, https://nymag.com/intelligencer/2020/12/cdc-drug-overdose-deaths-in-2020-on-track-to-break-record.html.

and ourselves on practices that improve outcomes. This may allow us to start *preventing* SUD, emergencies, and sequelae in place of providing crisis care.

We are not alone in this fight. Together, we can build a coalition to fight addiction. We've been working tirelessly to make this vision a reality. Through our four principal concepts—clinical utility, technology-assisted care, behavioral health equity, and patient engagement—we can optimize population health through risk stratification, closure of care gaps, facilitation of care coordination and care transitions, and identification of disease progression and regression. We can also reduce the total cost of care.

> **We are not alone in this fight.**

Through the use of technology and the implementation of key performance metrics, organizations will be empowered to automate and standardize clinical workflows, track performance using agreed-upon outcome and process metrics, and relieve saturated clinical care efforts. This will allow for the advancement of evidence-based care management and support the clinical utility of our collective efforts.

At the center of the current state of care are the substantial gaps in the equity of behavioral health access and care delivery. Systematic and programmatic responses can alleviate baked-in-the-cake biases in our healthcare structure and support a broad-based improvement in our coordinated efforts.

Finally, patients must be front and center. They, along with their loved ones, need to feel supported and empowered and be drivers of their own successes. This will help strong clinical efforts translate into lasting results.

We went into the healthcare field with the single desire to help others. Even back then, we saw substantial challenges within our field: compromises on how much time we could spend with patients; judicious use of healthcare resources to keep costs down; difficulties related to technology infrastructure and adoption; and behavioral health, which dictates so much of our wellness, being treated mostly independently of many other parts of our care delivery models.

In many ways we have come so far. There is now a priority to provide behavioral health, an acknowledgement of patient-centered care within the system as well as continued models for improving financial stewardship. Unfortunately, there is still much work to do. With structural changes to the insurance industry and legislative reforms—as well as a public awareness of behavioral health—we are poised to embrace not only a more holistic approach to clinical care but also a more comprehensive care delivery to the whole person.

As the world grapples with the COVID-19 pandemic, we have once again witnessed the humbling power of the uncontrollable aspect of the natural order of the world. We must research, find solutions to these health emergencies, and recognize that there are variables that may lie beyond our immediate control. But SUD care is not one of those uncontrollable situations. We can rally around a collective approach that draws the patient out from the shadows and into mainstream care. For the moment, however, the pandemic has sent us back a few steps. The number of SUDs, as well as suicides, have risen alarmingly during this difficult time, creating the need for improved protocols.

That effort begins with institutions maturing to new levels of providing care. The Institutional Achievement Index can provide organizations with metrics to assess where they are and how they can improve their offerings in a way that reflects the aims of this book—particularly in providing exceptional coordinated care.

This strategy emphasizes a few core principles: the urgent need for care coordination; an opportunity to leverage technology to surmount gaps in today's electronic health records; the ability to empower patients with educational services that meet them where they are; and finally, purpose-driven population-analytics tools to help manage care trends, assess risk proactively, and develop strategies to implement across your organization for long-term success.

We propose a systematic approach to stem the tide, improve outcomes, and drive costs down. However, we must recognize that as with any effective approach to chronic disease, early victories do not mean long-term success. Management of SUD over the long term must be the ultimate goal. As Winston Churchill famously stated after a victory in World War II, "It is not even the beginning of the end. But it is, perhaps, the end of the beginning."

Cam Lauf described his experiences trying to recover from his own SUD condition. Cam won that fight—and now he's fighting for others to do the same. In his words,

> This is what I do for a living now—I talk to people about their substance use concerns. And I counsel family members. My recent position was the supervisor to the Emergency Department's recovery coaching program at the University of Vermont Medical Center. And we would really just educate people about the severity of their use, the impact on their family members' use and also a realistic explanation of what to expect moving forward.
>
> But the reality is, it's a partnership. Recovery is a partnership from the individual to whatever their treatment options are to whatever their recovery options are. It has to be a

partnership and partnerships are best when the individual meets the other person halfway, or where they are.

Inspiring people like Cam represent significant wins in our struggle for a healthy society. Yes, we rejoice not only in his victory but also in all the victories we've achieved in our battles with SUD. At the same time, we realize we are only beginning to see just how innovative methods can create meaningful long-term change. Frankly, this represents an opportunity for everyone in the public and private sector to join in this fight. We need people and organizations that will reach beyond outdated and ineffective approaches, that are willing to change the paradigm from social and moral affliction to chronic disease management, and invite families, communities, unique care models, and risk sharing into the all-important ongoing conversation that will lead us to long-term success.

There are lives to be saved and good business to be had. We ask that you join us.

EPILOGUE

As we have shared, there is an increased need for organizational scale, coordination, and resources to effectively combat the current SUD epidemic. We have outlined how, in a fragmented care setting, we can improve outcomes and reduce costs by coordinating across the multiple critical care settings to which patients travel to effectively receive the best care possible. We have provided insights into how individual organizations can improve their process and evaluate where they are on the journey to comprehensive, collaborative care. Finally, we have discussed ways to better coordinate that care across multiple organizations.

At Aspenti Health, we have worked to develop, implement, and lead change and establish a strong thought leadership position. It became abundantly clear in a healthcare setting as complex and distributed as behavioral health that we needed reach and scale to connect across the vast number of players in our space. To continue and accelerate these efforts, we embarked on a process to find a partner through which we would be able to have an extended reach along with the organizational capacity to deliver on our promise of leading care change in the behavioral health ecosystem. As of June 2021, we combined our business through acquisition by an established organization with similar values and care goals called Averhealth. We are excited for this transition and the opportunities to bridge Averhealth's predominant focus on the judicial system with Aspenti Health's mission. While there are early adopters and change agents in our segment of healthcare, they are difficult to find, and we are grateful to have found a like-minded organization.

Millions and millions of dollars are distributed each year to organizations to support care, but few drive new models that deliver improved outcomes. In our current system, money is allocated across too many organizations and the parameters of this distribution remain ill defined. Our current delivery model heightens the critical role of the for-profit organization in the story line and evolution of clinical and business processes in SUD care. Local primary care doctors, specialized addiction care settings, large health systems, community care organizations, insurance providers, regulators, laboratories, software companies, and government payers all create a difficult web to navigate with any agility unless there is scale. We must move the needle forward and implore you to consider the changes we have outlined in this book. Together we can and must navigate among the many different players required to transform this industry. We need an injection of capital, an appetite to scale, and a grounded understanding of this space.

> Together we can and must navigate among the many different players required to transform this industry.

The stakes are high: the lives of an often underserved, vulnerable patient population that has been stigmatized and marginalized for far too long are on the line. The very fabric of society is at risk. May our collective journey begin. We hope you will join us in real change to create lasting recovery going forward.

SELF-ASSESSMENT: INSTITUTIONAL ACHIEVEMENT INDEX

Provider: _____

Organization: _____

Date of Completion: _____

Instructions: *For each question, select the description that best represents your organization. Tally the points from each question at the end of each section. Crosswalk the score to the individual level, and fill in the table directly below. The average of the four levels will determine the overall maturity index level.*

CORE COMPETENCIES	LEVEL
Collaborative Stewardship	
Evidence-Based Care	
Chronic Care Management	
Patient Engagement	
Maturity Index Level *(Sum levels above/4)*	

A. COLLABORATIVE STEWARDSHIP

1. *Do you have any overarching leadership or governance to support the management of substance use disorder (SUD) or behavioral health (BH)?*

    a. No overarching leadership or governance drives SUD management (1 pt).

    b. A nascent organizational governance or leadership has been established (2 pts).

    c. Effective leadership and/or governance is driving collaboration (3 pts).

    d. There is effective leadership and/or governance with established care teams (4 pts).

e. Leadership and/or governance is developing program initiatives that drive success (5 pts).

f. Leadership and/or governance and care teams are functioning as a single integrated program (6 pts).

2. *How do you coordinate across the organization in the management of individual patients?*

a. Most providers provide optimal care individually (1 pt).

b. Care is sporadically coordinated across the care continuum (2 pts).

c. Providers communicate routinely regarding specific patients (3 pts).

d. Providers communicate routinely regarding specific patients and collaborate on quality-improvement initiatives (4 pts).

e. Providers communicate across team members spanning medical, behavioral health, and community organizations (5 pts).

f. Providers and care team members share a single, unified vision and coordinate care routinely across all disciplines (6 pts).

3. *What mechanisms facilitate provider-based communications across the organization?*

a. There are no interdisciplinary provider-based communications (1 pt).

b. The organization primarily focuses on individual patient needs, leveraging interdisciplinary coordination as needed (2 pts).

c. Periodic collaborative meetings exist to understand one another's workflow and expertise (3 pts).

d. Care teams meet routinely to identify opportunities and quality improvements (4 pts).

e. Routine meetings of care teams consider a holistic approach to care delivery (5 pts).

f. Routine meetings of care teams commonly approach improvements to care delivery holistically and in an interdisciplinary way (6 pts).

4. *What mechanisms do you have in place to monitor programmatic progress or impact?*

a. Our institution focuses on the delivery of direct patient care (1 pt).

b. Our organization has a few key performance indicators that are tracked for regulatory purposes, but they are not widely available/visible and don't routinely inform quality-improvement projects (2 pts).

c. Broadly available performance indicators and/or dashboards have been discussed but not implemented (3 pts).

d. Our organization has instituted performance indicators, and they are available to all. But only leadership uses them (4 pts).

e. Performance indicators are used to show incremental improvements in targets (5 pts).

f. Performance indicators are used to identify opportunities for ongoing improvements in care, and impact is demonstrated through these mechanisms (6 pts).

5. *What health payment models predominate?*

    a. Our organization and the services we provide are exclusively fee-for-service (1 pt).

    b. Fee-for-service health payment models predominate within our organization (2 pts).

    c. Fee-for-service health payment models predominate; however, we are trialing value-based reimbursement models (3 pts).

    d. Our organization has committed to some value-based care delivery (4 pts).

    e. We have adopted a value-based care model but continue to work through risk adjustments at our institution (5 pts).

    f. We have fully adopted a value-based care model, and risk-adjustment determinations are well honed within our institution (6 pts).

Score for Collaborative Stewardship

QUESTION #	CATEGORY	SCORE (POINTS)
1	Leadership/governance	1 2 3 4 5 6
2	Care coordination	1 2 3 4 5 6
3	Communication	1 2 3 4 5 6
4	Monitoring	1 2 3 4 5 6
5	Payment models	1 2 3 4 5 6
Total score		1–5: Level 1 6–10: Level 2 11–15: Level 3 16–20: Level 4 21–25: Level 5 26–30: Level 6

B. EVIDENCE-BASED CARE

1. *What is the capacity of a qualified provider for managing patients with SUDs?*

    a. We have experienced substantial gaps in provider capacity—both in prescribing providers and counseling. The organization has no formal estimate on need and capacity (1 pt).

    b. While access to buprenorphine-waived providers has increased, the organization still struggles with gaps in counseling and therapy. The organization has no formal estimate on need and capacity (2 pts).

    c. The organization has begun to define its capacity and needs for SUD providers. Substantial work in recruiting appropriate resources is needed (3 pts).

    d. The organization is actively recruiting personnel to fill resource gaps that have been identified in SUD care (4 pts).

    e. Our organization has largely identified and filled resource gaps to support SUD care; however, we do not have a standard mechanism to track capacity shifts for the future (5 pts).

    f. Our institution has sufficient resources to provide SUD care. We have developed ongoing mechanisms to track capacity shifts and needs (6 pts).

2. *What has been the extent of targeted provider training related to SUD topics?*

    a. Our institution has not had sufficient resources to provide additional training on SUD specifically (1 pt).

b. We have leveraged some provider training resources to support care of opioid use disorder (including delivery of MAT care, opioid prescribing, and use of naloxone); however, we have difficulty culling material to find what is most useful to our staff (2 pts).

c. We have committed a specific resource within our institution to identify relevant course material and training to introduce staff to expanding SUD and behavioral-health topics (3 pts).

d. A committed resource works with our local community to identify training opportunities on the topics of SUD and behavioral health (4 pts).

e. Providers describe themselves as confident in SUD and BH care and receive sufficient community resources for SUD and behavioral health topics (5 pts).

f. Providers are confident in the delivery of SUD and BH care, receive ongoing training on these topics, and committed resources ensure training and competencies in this area are tracked (6 pts).

3. *Are standardized protocols, policies, and resources developed for the SUD population and used across the organization?*

a. We provide the best individualized care possible. Standardized policies, protocols, and resources have not been developed to support the SUD population (1 pt).

b. Standard policies, protocols, and/or resources for SUD care have been developed, but no substantial adoption has been seen (2 pts).

c. Some adoption and use of standard policies, protocols, and common resources have been seen; however, the very limited use tends to be restricted to those who created the protocols and not observed widely (3 pts).

d. Standard policies, protocols, and resources are easily accessed, and some use of these common strategies is seen. Providers express some discomfort over prescriptive approaches (4 pts).

e. Easily accessed and standardized protocols and resources are commonly and broadly used. Providers express comfort with use, and all are aligned with where individualized care intersects with standard processes (5 pts).

f. Easily accessed and standardized protocols and resources are commonly and broadly used. Providers express comfort with use, and all are aligned with where individualized care intersects with standard processes. Mechanisms exist to routinely update and modify processes to improve care (6 pts).

4. *Have care gaps and/or transitions of care been identified, mapped, and addressed?*

a. Individual care gaps and/or transitions of care have yet to be identified (1 pt).

b. Care gaps are beginning to be mapped. Insufficient resources exist to work to close gaps and improve transitions of care (2 pts).

c. The clinical practice recognizes the importance of a holistic care model for SUD and BH and expresses specific interest in improving care gaps and transitions of care. The care gaps and transitions in care are being mapped (3 pts).

d. We have mapped the gaps in care along the SUD care continuum from prevention to management of disease progression, comorbidities, and disease sequelae. We are developing mechanisms to address these care gaps (4 pts).

e. The program has identified care gaps/care transitions with specific quality-improvement initiatives in progress to address. Institution has initiated steps to manage patients holistically with anticipation of and identification of comorbidities and disease sequelae (5 pts).

f. Care gaps and/or transitions have been targeted with integrated care teams managing through transitions of care. Patients are managed holistically with anticipation of and identification of comorbidities and disease sequelae (6 pts).

5. *Has the practice incorporated social determinants of health into care delivery?*

a. Social determinants of health have not been addressed within our care organization (1 pt).

b. The organization wants to incorporate social determinants of health but has not yet executed this improvement (2 pts).

c. Social determinants of health are addressed in an ad hoc fashion and are targeted to support clinical management (such as gas cards to get patients to their appointment) (3 pts).

d. Social determinants of health are asked of patients, but information largely resides in medical records, without action (4 pts).

e. Social determinants of health are tracked on a population level but have not been systematically integrated into care plans but instead inform quality-improvement projects (5 pts).

f. Social determinants of health are tracked on a population level and directly inform individual care (6 pts).

Score for Evidence-Based Care:

QUESTION #	CATEGORY	SCORE (POINTS)
1	Capacity	1 2 3 4 5 6
2	Training	1 2 3 4 5 6
3	Protocols	1 2 3 4 5 6
4	Care gaps/transitions	1 2 3 4 5 6
5	Social determinants	1 2 3 4 5 6
Total score		1–5: Level 1 6–10: Level 2 11–15: Level 3 16–20: Level 4 21–25: Level 5 26–30: Level 6

C. CHRONIC DISEASE MANAGEMENT

1. *Is SUD seen and treated like other chronic diseases within the organization?*

   a. We do not treat SUD as a chronic disease but focus more on episodic progress through an individual's care (1 pt).

   b. We recognize that SUD is a chronic disease, but it is managed differently from other chronic diseases (2 pts).

   c. Our institution's leadership has recognized the importance of SUD as being managed as a chronic disease; however, we have not determined mechanisms to modify the care delivery to address this model (3 pts).

   d. A chronic disease model perspective influences our care delivery and considers the entire spectrum of care from prevention to early diagnosis to anticipation of chronic disease sequelae and comorbidities (4 pts).

   e. The chronic care model is fully embraced for SUD care and mirrors that of any other chronic disease managed at our institution; however, mechanisms to track success in comparison to other diseases remain ill defined (5 pts).

   f. The chronic care model is fully embraced for SUD care and mirrors that of any other chronic disease managed at our institution. Performance indicators, such as treatment retention and adherence, match that of other chronic diseases (6 pts).

2. *Does the organization employ prevention strategies to manage patients at risk for SUD and/or sequelae?*

a. Our organization is focused on SUD care delivery and not prevention efforts (1 pt).

b. Our organization's leadership has discussed prevention as a necessary part of our strategic goals; however, we have few standardized resources (2 pts).

c. We have developed some resources to support prevention efforts for patients at risk for SUD; however, we do not track how these are used (3 pts).

d. Prevention efforts for individuals at risk for SUD are an important focus of our organization with standardized resources. We expect these resources are well used but do not monitor use (4 pts).

e. At our organization, prevention efforts span those at risk for SUD as well as those at risk for SUD sequelae. We have some standardized resources for the former but not the latter. We track use of resources (5 pts).

f. There is a system-wide emphasis on prevention and early diagnosis, with well-developed, standardized resources. We track use of these resources (6 pts).

3. *Is a population health model used to stratify patients' risk in terms of SUD?*

a. We provide care on an individual basis and do not have the means to track patients at a population level (1 pt).

b. We provide individualized care. While we capture broad analytics for regulatory and/or operational purposes, we do not use this data to drive patient care (2 pts).

c. A population health approach has unveiled some risk categories among our patients, but there has been no adoption in care management (3 pts).

d. We have begun to categorize patients using population health analytics. Efforts have been mostly claims based (4 pts).

e. We have found that early risk stratification is becoming an integral part of care management (5 pts).

f. Risk stratification of subpopulations is intrinsic to our institution's care delivery (6 pts).

4. *Has the organization constructed a center of excellence or coordinated program around SUD?*

a. Our organization does not have the capacity for constructing a coordinated program around SUD (1 pt).

b. We have limited integration of care across the spectrum of diseases that pertain to SUD and pain patients (2 pts).

c. We have some integration of services across pain, SUD, and SUD sequelae, with few shared resources across different disciplines (3 pts).

d. We have integration of services across pain, SUD, and SUD sequelae, with several shared resources (4 pts).

e. Leadership is considering a formal center of excellence; however, the programmatic efforts are still in progress (5 pts).

f. We have a fully integrated delivery of care across pain, SUD, and SUD sequelae, with shared resources and a programmatic approach (6 pts).

5. *Are harm-reduction strategies used?*

   a. We have an abstinence model and are not centered on harm reduction (1 pt).

   b. We consider buprenorphine and methadone as sufficient harm-reduction strategies (2 pts).

   c. We recognize the importance of harm reduction but have insufficient resources to keep abreast of emerging new strategies (3 pts).

   d. Harm-reduction strategies are commonly considered in care (4 pts).

   e. Harm-reduction strategies are commonly used and integrated into care (5 pts).

   f. We fully embrace the harm-reduction model and deploy a diverse array of strategies that are fully integrated into care (6 pts).

Score for Chronic Disease Management:

QUESTION #	CATEGORY	SCORE (POINTS)
1	Recognition of chronic disease	1 2 3 4 5 6
2	Prevention	1 2 3 4 5 6
3	Population health approach	1 2 3 4 5 6
4	Centers of excellence	1 2 3 4 5 6
5	Harm reduction	1 2 3 4 5 6
Total score		1–5: Level 1 6–10: Level 2 11–15: Level 3 16–20: Level 4 21–25: Level 5 26–30: Level 6

D. PATIENT ENGAGEMENT

1. *Has the organization adopted strategies to empower patients and/or loved ones in patient care?*

   a. Patients are part of their care, receiving basic services of access of health information through patient portals and as part of clinical decision-making (1 pt).

   b. We have considered ways to empower and engage patients and families but have been limited in our ability to execute these initiatives (2 pts).

   c. Strategies and specific mechanisms to empower and engage patients are developed and actively used but largely centered around educational opportunities rather than seeking input in our practice (3 pts).

   d. Strategies and specific mechanisms to empower and engage patients are developed and actively used. These strategies may affect our clinical practice. We have not effectively reached out to seek family input (4 pts).

   e. Patient- and family-oriented engagement strategies inform clinical care; however, we are reliant upon a vocal few to inform our work (5 pts).

   f. Patients and families are actively engaged in their care, informing treatment algorithms, facility improvements, and design and access discussions. Patient diversity is heavily weighted in decisions (6 pts).

2. *Has the organization introduced patient advisory groups or patient ambassadors into care settings?*

a. Patient advisory groups or patient ambassadors and family members have not been introduced into care settings (1 pt).

b. We are considering the addition of patient advisory groups or patient ambassadors in advisory roles (2 pts).

c. Patient advisory groups or patient ambassadors are being recruited for involvement in care settings; family members have not been part of the scope of this work (3 pts).

d. Patient advisory groups or patient ambassadors are part of care settings; families have not been incorporated into care discussions (4 pts).

e. Patient advisory groups or patient ambassadors promote changes in care to improve patient experience. Family members are incorporated into advisory settings (5 pts).

f. Patient advisory groups or patient ambassadors promote changes in care to improve patient experience. Family members are incorporated into advisory settings and drive changes in care (6 pts).

3. *Are the organization's patients able to trend or track progress in their care?*

a. Patient access to clinical information is limited to discrete episodes of care (1 pt).

b. Patient access to clinical information is extended to web-based portals and minimal targeted literature / educational content (2 pts).

c. Patient access to clinical information is extended to web-based portals and some targeted literature/educational content (3 pts).

d. Patient access to clinical information is extended to web-based portals and extensive targeted literature / educational content (4 pts).

e. Patient and family access to clinical information includes web-based portals, targeted literature / educational content, and innovative ways to address questions and needs in real time (5 pts).

f. Patient and family access to clinical information includes web-based portals, targeted literature / educational content, and innovative ways to address questions and needs in real time (6 pts).

4. *Has the organization determined whether patients themselves feel empowered in their own care?*

a. We have not surveyed or asked patients whether they feel empowered (1 pt).

b. While we have surveyed patients and/or families about whether they feel empowered in their care, discovery efforts indicate that patients view themselves as passive recipients of care (2 pts).

c. Surveys and/or feedback demonstrates that patients are beginning to see themselves as champions of their own care (3 pts).

d. Patients see themselves as champions of their own care. They do not see their role as informing others' care. They see some strategies to engage loved ones on their behalf (4 pts).

e. Patients see themselves as champions of their own care and are beginning to see the role they can play in informing others' care. They see some strategies to engage loved ones on their behalf (5 pts).

f. Patients are champions of their own care and drive quality-improvement changes in care settings for their own and others' benefit. They are able to engage family members for their benefit (6 pts).

5. *Does the organization leverage technology—including smartphones—to empower access and care management in the field of SUD?*

a. The organization has not adopted technology as a solution for patients and/or families (1 pt).

b. The organization has a patient portal available to all patients (2 pts).

c. In addition to a patient portal, the organization uses text messaging for appointment scheduling if requested by the patient (3 pts).

d. The organization is exploring use of smartphones or other strategies to communicate and disseminate medical findings (4 pts).

e. The organization has recently introduced a technology to communicate with patients and/or family members, to disseminate findings, and to leverage patient and family resources specific to SUD (5 pts).

f. Technology has been a long-standing mechanism to communicate with patients and/or family members, to provide clinical information, and to provide additional resources, such as education (6 pts).

Score for Patient Engagement:

QUESTION #	CATEGORY	SCORE (POINTS)
1	Strategies of empowerment	1 2 3 4 5 6
2	Patient advisors/ ambassadors	1 2 3 4 5 6
3	Tracking progress	1 2 3 4 5 6
4	Soliciting feedback	1 2 3 4 5 6
5	Technology	1 2 3 4 5 6
Total score		1–5: Level 1 6–10: Level 2 11–15: Level 3 16–20: Level 4 21–25: Level 5 26–30: Level 6

GAP ANALYSIS TEMPLATE

Organization: _____

Date of Completion: _____

Instructions: *For the Landscape & Current State column, consider responses in your self-assessment tool. As demonstrated in the example, you can copy responses from the self-assessment to complete the first column. For the Gap, consider the higher scores within that question as to what gaps you may have. An example is shown.*

GAP ANALYSIS TEMPLATE					
Landscape & Current State	Gap	Solves How	Outcome	Measurable Impact	Source of Insights
We provide care on an individual basis and do not have the means to track patients at a population level (1 pt). (Chronic disease C.3).	We can't track patients at a population level.	Implementation of a population health management tool (technology-assisted care).	**Operational:** ability to risk stratify patients by disease severity Clinical: segregate high-risk population to identify acute care utilization. **Financial:** determine cost associated with high-risk acute care use.	Assess numbers of patients in high-risk disease severity; determine attributable cost of acute care events.	Self-assessment tools by 2 MDs, 3 social workers, and 1 executive.

PROGRAM CHARTER TEMPLATE			
PROJECT/PROGRAM TITLE:			
PROJECT SPONSOR(S):		**PROJECT MANAGER:**	
DATE OF PROJECT APPROVAL:		**LAST REVISION DATE:**	
PROJECT PURPOSE STATEMENT:			
BUSINESS CASE / GOALS:			
Benefit Statements:	Clinical:	Internal:	
		External:	
	Financial:	Internal:	
		External:	
	Operational:	Internal:	
		External:	
Project Deliverables:			
Benefits: (measurable results)	KPI:	Baseline:	Goal:
Estimated ROI:			
Constraints: (in priority order)	Time/Duration:		
	Budget:		
	Scope:	What is the problem we are attempting to solve?:	
		What is in scope?:	
		What is out of scope?:	
	Quality:		

Governance:	Steering Committee:	Project Team:
	CEO:	Program Manager:
	CFO:	IDN Lead:
	Clinical Champion:	Data Analytics Lead:
	Population Health Lead:	IT Lead:
Key Stakeholders	Name:	Success Criteria:
Risks:		

KICKOFF MEETING TEMPLATE

Project Name: _____

Project Sponsor: _____

Project Owner: _____

Date: _____

TOPIC	TIME ALLOTTED
Introductions and welcome—*Project Owner*	10 minutes
Orientation to project—*Project Sponsor* 1) Why we are committing to this project and what needs to change 2) High-level scope requirements 3) 1–3 critical success metrics 4) Identification of key stakeholders	10 minutes
Present project objectives—*Project Owner* 1) Assumptions 2) Objectives 3) Deliverables	10 minutes
Identify operating mechanisms—*Project Owner* 1) Highlight key stakeholders. 2) Assign committees and/or teams, as applicable. 3) Determine meeting cadence.	10 minutes
Facilitate discussion—*Project Owner* 1) Allow for team discussion. 2) Q&A	10–15 minutes
Review next steps and action items—*Project Owner* 1) Summarize action items. 2) Schedule the next meeting.	5 minutes

PROJECT IMPLEMENTATION PLAN TEMPLATE

Project Name: _____

Project Sponsor: _____

Project Owner: _____

PROJECT CHARACTERISTICS	PROJECT DESCRIPTION
Overview:	
Vision	
Mission	
Objective	
Assumptions & limitations	
Scope	
Project team:	
Sponsor	
Owner/manager	
Steering committee members (if applicable)	
Key team members	
Other stakeholders	
Implementation schedule:	
Project milestones	
Project timelines	
Reporting tasks	
Resource management:	
Additional contributing individuals	
Equipment needs	
Software needs	
Other	
Success metrics:	
Operational metrics	
Quality metrics	

User satisfaction and knowledge	
Financial metrics	
Additional documentation:	

Approval: _____

Date: _____

QUARTERLY PROJECT REVIEW TEMPLATE

Project Name: _____

Project Sponsor: _____

Project Owner:_____

Project Objectives:_____

PROJECT CHARACTERISTICS	STATUS UPDATE
Project update: Identify successes and setbacks.	
Performance on key metrics: Operational metrics Financial/budgetary metrics Quality metrics Stakeholder satisfaction	
Gap analysis: Identification of areas that require additional improvements Highlight future state.	
Action items and next steps:	

WEB-BASED RESOURCES

Addiction Recovery Medical Home:
https://www.incentivizerecovery.org/

American Addiction Centers:
https://www.rehabs.com blog/6-common-family-roles-in-an-addicted-household/

SAMHSA:
https://www.samhsa.gov/

National Institute on Drug Abuse:
https://www.drugabuse.gov/

Phoenix House New England:
https://www.phoenixhousene.org/

BRC Healthcare:
https://brc-healthcare.com/

Averhealth:
https://averhealth.com

Sharon Wegscheider-Cruse, on the role of family in addiction:
https://familiesimpactedbyopioids.com/

Centers for Disease Control and Prevention:
https://www.cdc.gov/pwid/addiction.html

American Society of Addiction Medicine:
https://www.asam.org/

CPSIA information can be obtained
at www.ICGtesting.com
Printed in the USA
JSHW050502260422
25280JS00010B/20